Seek

Katie McCreary

authorHOUSE®

AuthorHouse™
1663 Liberty Drive
Bloomington, IN 47403
www.authorhouse.com
Phone: 1 (800) 839-8640

All scriptures taken from King James Version of the Bible.

Published by AuthorHouse 10/20/2017

ISBN: 978-1-5462-1283-6 (sc)
ISBN: 978-1-5462-1282-9 (e)

Print information available on the last page.

SECTION ONE

Preface

John 15:16 " Ye have not chosen me, but I have chosen you, and ordained you, that ye should go and bring forth fruit, and that your fruit should remain: that whatsoever ye shall ask of the father in my name, he may give it you."

God started speaking to me in 2012. I knew this was God because the voice was within me, even audible at time but only to my own ears. As I started seeking more of God through his word, I would find the things and even exact words he would say to me. I knew this was proof, as well as the way the Holy Spirit was going to train my ear up in knowing his voice. God told me I was an end time prophet, and after many years of waiting on prophecy from God, he finally revealed to me saying *"Katie you seek Me and you seek Me with your whole heart and you have found Me in my secret place, you have found Me in my Holy Manifold. You truly know Me. You seek Me in your prison, and trusted me in your confusion. Now your love for Me has been made perfect. Tell my story and how I have loved you. Tell them how much*

1

*I love them as I have loved you. Prophesy Me to the confused, and the abused, and unto the ridiculed and one who ridicules. Speak My peace, and prophesy My truths, that it may set the captives free and give them hope. Can you not realize that you were meant for greatness? Now suit up! Time waits for no one! It is time to be a prophet. Now let down your guard, **I AM** in charge now!"*

Yes, this was my call from God! I realized I would be a prophet of The Great Elohim to minister of his own heart unto his creation, because he has trusted in me with his own heart, not only to prophesy about it, but to minister from out of his own heart. His heart that is now mine. Many can witness His unfailing love, but only His true beloved can hold all the pain, the sorrow, and grief that holds a power all its own. I have been put in a battlefield, a love story, a love song, that knows everything there is to know about loving God! Every battle cry, every happy ending, and every love note, pitch, and key. Am I special? Well I guess maybe I am. It sure feels like it, to hold the secrets of The Living God. But I do know one thing. It's only as wonderful as I make it, and that grace is what allows me to hold hands and share a perfect heart with specifically who **I AM**; not who I was or wasn't.

Sorry if it seems as if I'm bragging, and whether it is or isn't, I have no shame because I know we should not gloat in worldly things, but to boast in the glory of the Lord and how we know Him, even the more we know Him, as long as He lives, and give thanks, and recompense to this unfailing love!

I got to admit I do feel a little handpicked, or tinctured by his personal flavor. Well, why wouldn't I? I've awakened with opened eyes, amongst all the blindfolded eyes. I've been witness to multitudes of spiritual discernments and been given authority to rebuke demonic spirits by the thousands by the hand of the one who saves! So whether I save people or whether I don't, I don't have to congratulate myself because I'm already honored!

I don't consider myself religious or self-existent. I believe I have been made a spiritual being by God's Spirit, in order to experience life on a human level, as well as life among the spiritual realm. I believe Earth is a very expensive schooling for our maturing and transforming souls, as well as a very short hotel stay. We are all on a journey called life, set in different places, at different levels, and some with spiritual experiences, because we are created remarkably in Christ who strengthens us to be remarkable through Christ.

I believe with all my being, that with every amazing creation, there is an even more wondrous creator. This is my experience with my Creator. For even my story is **His'** **s**tory, because **His'** story is **His**-tory.

Hebrews 5:12

You have been believers so long now that you ought to be teaching others. Instead, you need someone to teach you again the basic things about God's word. You are like babies who need milk and cannot eat solid food.

I don't consider myself a motivational speaker, unless your definition of a motivational speaker is someone who lights a fire under your butt. I've noticed most people like their motivation raw and I don't mean in " beast ala- mode " but more like untouched and untendered, which is not a good thing for meat eaters. I know I like my meat so tender it might hit a nerve! How about you? When I do offer motivation, I like to light a match and serve mine up with fire to make sure it gets baked in, but one thing I won't do is cut your meat for you, meat is supposed to be served solid and uncut, there's a lot of beauty in it that way. Good meat is always seasoned and well prepared with flare. As the saying goes "you are what you eat" maybe that's why I like my meat well done and rough around the edges, but I would never serve you something that I wouldn't eat myself. Better yet if you eat what I eat, you would be eating prime rib from the Lord's Holy Manifold! (in layman terms.) No man gains weight on milk alone but by the very Word of God.

Bone Appetite!

Introduction

There was an exceptional woman who truly knew and loved her King. She witnessed true love and all the exceptional things. Heaven had brought His Majesty His soulmate. They were inseparable. Blinded by His glorious face, she tells Him " I'll see you later" yet they were always together, and they were always worth it. Bad choices and sin were always popping up. Step by step, and bit by bit, but she was always beautiful to Him. Their chemistry was marvelous, everything was perfect, with or without sin separating them faithfully, or driving a wedge until faithful didn't feel so wonderful, that's when faithful was only a mystery, and forgiveness didn't seem like the way home until Faithful was His dying name.

The gift of true unfailing love is of no practical magic, no fairy dust, and of course nothing in any chapter book that can explain what is truly president about our transformation when your elected unto the 144,000 saints, to keep our robes clean without spot or blemish, holy, and without blame.

The Holy grail of partnership is not an overstatement when referencing to what this romantic couple shares.

No fairy tales could prove truly; what true love is all about. Even the weak fall in love with the strong, and the strong fall in love with the weakest of souls! I say with certainty that no child is perfect, but when they get older they put away their childish things and strive for peace on earth. Everybody is worthy of finding their innocence and their true love, by heaven's mistake; God's rejection.

So as destiny becomes true, no one and nothing more should ever have quenched her beautiful soul's relinquishments, that are fueled by passion and God's own Son.

And He was more than a Savior to her, more and more. More than her one-way ticket to paradise. The more He conquered her sins, love's certainty moved, and moved, and moved! Each and every morning, noon, and night, she fell empty, over pouring her own heart into her King. So with much gratitude He carried her wherever she was more than willing to go, and thankfully he was more than willing to take her with him closely. Just as close as you could find two love birds, was as certain as the Holy Spirit would take them forever deep, where time has no meaning. Still timing would orchestrate for resonating with perfect sounds, just as deep as they could go; they would go. No love should go unanswered where trust waits for perfect love; essentially.

The key to answering by the Holy Spirit of God is in this riddle; time waits for no one person, but if you wait on somebody else's own personal and faithful time, then miracles happen because time stands still and is actually optional, then and only then does eternity become symmetrical with Heaven.

There are two answers to the understanding of this holy conundrum that her King explained fervently to her: "time waits for no one person, but if someone waits on someone else's time, then time has nowhere to go but to wait on someone else's time.

The second understanding is this; "time waits on no one, but if someone waits on someone else's time, then time has nowhere to go, but to wait on someone who waits on someone else's time."

So each time they met she gave her heart and soul to the one she called true love and true happiness, with true passion and mirth. At last her once unfaithful heart was perfected by the Great Perfector!

His own perfect heart ministers love and provisions of what true love should look and feel like. His heart ministers how perfect and in love they truly are.

Then one fateful and true day, she collapsed in her own heart, all at once they were bounded together by her surrender. The look and feel is good when the moment comes, when each and every breath they take comes from the same heart, her new heart which is bound to be yours some rigorous and patiently awaited day.

Since this is a true story I am proud to say every chance you get, do it with a new heart, because you don't always know when your heart will beat again from that same place, or where true love's heart will beat from.

SECTION THREE

The Deepest Love

1 John 19 We love him because He loved us first.

John 15:13 Greater love hath no man then this that a man lay down his life for his friends.

The agape love of God is manifested through God's only begotten son. A love that is truly a witness to God's unfailing love. God's love is like the ocean. Let me explain the visual eloquence of God's love. Can you picture the ocean and the white sand, with waves crashing all over? Now imagine you are afraid of getting wet, so you walk out to catch the waves with just your toes. Eventually you get used to it, it feels good to your toes so you go a little farther. "Oh this isn't bad, what was I afraid of?" So you start to chase the water when it retracts to the ocean, again and again you play "tug of war " and you realize, "boy this is remarkable! I better cool off just a little bit longer." Next thing you know your swimming right past her. Oh who's the gal letting the wind and waves sweep her away? It's me of course! Hey you don't get to Heaven by yourself! There's millions of us swimming around here, in our own sweet surrender. (wink wink). Isn't it sweet?

You can surf the waves, float, or search the depths trying to find all there is to find. Nobody minds. They are all on their own currents, literally.

Whatever path you find, they're all in the same ocean. AKA God's amazing, unfathomable love. Just have fun and let him direct "the motion of the ocean!"

Let's move along. The Lords amazing love is like the ocean's depth in an uncanny way. The mystery of who He is and who He isn't, would blow you out of the water!

Job 11:7-12. "Can you fathom the mysteries of God? Can you probe the limits of The Almighty? They are higher than The Heavens Above - what can you do? They are deeper than The Depths Below - what can you know? The measures are longer then the earth and wider than the sea."

MOTION -" God moves in a mysterious way. His wonders to preform/ He plants His footsteps in The Sea/ and rides upon The Storm. (poem by William Cowper).

John 4:14 " but whoever drinks of the water that I will give him shall never thirst;

but the water that I shall give him shall be in him a well of water springing up into everlasting life."

God's unchanging love is to us as The Living Waters are with the raging ocean.

Where can we go but deeper, deeper and deeper? There is no greater love then His true, unchanging, uncanny, predestined, romantic, breathtaking, infinite love!

Just as the ocean cleanses and is self-sustaining, God's love cleanses us from sin and impurity.

Zechariah 13:1-9 is a profound example of how God cleanses. Being that God is the very essence, element, nature, and expression of love. He is self-sustaining and extends to you and I. Love finds Love, as ocean meets ocean. Consistently. The Lord compasses all the oceans, making certain they never stop or slow down.

Proverbs 8:27 "when He prepared the Heavens I was there: when He set a compass on the face of The Depth."

The more the Lord draws us in to His magnetic love, the tides change. Ironically the deeper we are in this ocean (love) the safer we are. Besides you can't do any whale watching or anything worth seeking in the harbor. The power of the ocean emanates from the middle, and literally creates a tunnel just for love. Whether you are sucked in or drawn in, the thing about the ocean (God's love) is you will eventually get to where you're going, no matter what you're going through.

If God brings you to it, He will lead you through it.

Philippians 1:6 " being confidant of this very thing that He which hath begun a good work in you will perform it until the day of Jesus Christ."

As ocean gives life to ocean, marine life gives back in which they swam for.

Section Four

Love

1 Corinthians 13:4-8

4 Love is patient, love is kind. It does not envy, it does not boast, it is not proud. 5 It does not dishonor others, it is not self-seeking, it is not easily angered, it keeps no record of wrongs. 6 Love does not delight in evil but rejoices with the truth. 7 It always protects, always trusts, always hopes, always perseveres. 8 Love never fails

Psalms 27: 8 " when you said seek my face my heart said to you " Your face Lord I will seek."

Jeremiah 29:13 "And ye shall seek me and find me, when ye shall search for me with all your heart."

Where is God and how do you find him? God's love is the strongest power, element, and substance that we can obtain, but what does obtain really mean?

How does one know where to begin and where to end the earnest seeking?

Well I can say this, you're only as smart as you are intelligent. That's the quickest I can explain confidence. Nobody is perfect at seeking anything. Not even the biggest holy roller can begin to take that leap of faith with carnal motives.

Carnal motives are for the carnal, which God is not.

Romans 8:5 " For they that are of the flesh set their minds on the things of the flesh, but those who are according to the Spirit, the things of the Spirit."

In order to obtain all the spiritual countenance, you must speak loud and clear in faith, for the things that your heart does desire. Whether it be in change, to know God, or to be a better listener. God has the ability to change any living soul according to His will. Good or bad. God doesn't deny or refuse any of you that come willingly to Christ. God has a purpose for everything that moves great and small, he even has the ability to change any sinner into a saint. God won't be the problem on any account! All you have to do is ask and believe with true faith, then you can consider it done!

James 4:2-3

2 Ye lust, and have not: ye kill, and desire to have, and cannot obtain: ye fight and war, yet ye have not, because ye ask not 3 Ye ask, and receive not, because ye ask amiss, that ye may consume it upon your lusts.

You labor upon a dunghill. You sow in riches of the earth and you think not of your spoiled hands. So do you ask God for things that would bring forth a salutation of some sorts, or to get to where Christ has gone, to paradise?

Then let's get personal!

God saves who God wants to save from perishing in The Valley of Dry Bones, and death.

2 Peter 3:9

9 The Lord is not slack concerning his promise, as some men count slackness; but is longsuffering to us-ward, not willing that any should perish, but that all should come to repentance.

God is capable, but free will is man's responsibility in not convicting him to an early grave. If you were dehydrated then you must experience uncomfortableness, inflammation, and a longing to be quenched of your thirst. If you fail to surrender to your impulses to rehydrate, then you quickly will be amongst the living dead, and perish for eternity. So wise up, we were not created for a challenge that doesn't have any reason or wrong doing. Your Confidant is The Holy Spirit and He will make sure you are ministered to faithfully and are totally confident in restoration. So let's make our move! To be prisoners of our Lord and not to free will. I include myself. As I'm ministering or writing. I am constantly learning on the same playing field, no lower no higher than any of you. The truth is not of our own reasoning in anyway. Trust me I know better than to believe my own carnal mind, being my own witness to this many times! Anyone who hears prophetically can testify, the words don't always come easy, and discerning everything is a necessity. There is no danger in finding your true love, only danger in not finding His love. Have no worries, central intelligence is who God is, and who the earth answers to! It's safe to say you're a diamond in the ruff and it's time for you to shine through.

True Love is not always having our hand out, with our hearts prepared to receive, which is most people's peril. True love requires sacrifices, because surrendered love is a whole different story. Most people have no peace. They may be happy over here and some over there, but that's not joy. If people knew true love, God's love, they would never compromise it, or trade it for measly happiness. People often feel taken advantage of by the word "love" but the truth is love is taken advantage of and not returned.

The Lord spoke to me saying;

"Daughter this world will never know happiness for what it is worth. This world has stolen many children's happiness, does it not show you who invented their happiness? What they invented they can certainly take away, but not up here!" said The Lord.

Faith

Romans 5:1 " Therefore having been justified by faith, we have peace with God through our Lord Jesus Christ whom also we have access by faith into His grace in which we stand and rejoice in hope of the glory of God."

The Lord is faithful to the faithless, but justifies the faithful. If faith can move mountains, then it's safe to say God is faithful unto faithful. The truth of the matter is if faith moves mountains and faith saves, that should show you who faith is. Faith can't do anything apart from God. Faith is no different from pride apart from who we are in Christ. Faith is who we are a part of, and not apart from the dispensation of the Holy Spirit. Just as love is not a part of us, love is who we are a part of!

1 John 4:7 " True Love comes from the Father, whoever has true love has God as His Father."

1 Corinthians 13:4-8, 4 Love is patient, love is kind. It does not envy, it does not boast, it is not proud. 5 It does not dishonor others, it is not self-seeking, it is not easily angered, it keeps no record of wrongs. 6 Love does not delight in evil but rejoices with the truth. 7 It always protects, always trusts, always hopes, always perseveres. 8 Love never fails.

Let me start by explaining that faith is the substance of things not seen, but belief is the substance of things seen and unseen. Therefore, faith is an understatement when it comes to someone's belief system, because faith doesn't know right or wrong if it believes in itself. Faith convinces faith, not faith convinces belief.

That's why in perfect love, faith casts out fear when nothing else can. Truly faith is the substance that orchestrates everything that love adheres to. Isn't it true what they say, that "there is no fear in love." 1 John 4:18? Of course it is, and isn't love true faith's admission by grace, or if you switch it around is not grace by faith's admission true love? Either way you look at it or switch it around, the bottle line is true love and faith go hand in hand, that's why true faith is love and love is true faith. If you knew the power of them together you would whimper instead of waiver in trusting God! Faith is trust, as true love is trust. Faith isn't always about who we are, as much as it is about who we are a part of; The Living God and Author of our faith, by who He says He is; our Love. Is our love a part of who He is, or who He actually is? Or is love so blinding that one cannot determine which one is the Father?

Since faith is true love and true love is only of the Father, then let me tell you why love is so blinding. Love (who God is) witnesses to our soul. Then our soul witnesses to our God of Heaven. So why is love so blinding? Because you would have to see it to believe it! The Bible says no one has seen God at any time except Jesus. His glory alone killed the men who looked in the Holy of Holies.

Even Moses had to wear a veil to conceal God's glory because he spoke with God. That's why faith is also recompense. Ha and you thought love was going to be easy! Surprise! All that you are depends on how you receive not perceive. That's why love is blinding because we wouldn't know it unless we felt it. Love doesn't have a physical look; it's not specified by sight in God's eyes. That's the reason He turns a "blind eye" to it, so He can hear what the heart has to say.

Discern all faith, not all faith is fair or just. Just faith is fair. There is faith based faith, which is "faith" in religion or practices which can be of the world and not of God. Here's a holy conundrum for you. Prove this, if eternal life is faith willed, then what kind of will does faith discern? If the same faith that can move mountains can be obtained by a mustard seed (so to speak) then why is every person of "faith" so stubborn? What kind of faith is that witnessing?

Faith witnesses to mercy, and faith also witnesses to our shame because faith witnesses to truth. However your story unfolds, we are still blind folded because of self-pity, backsliding, and being unrepentant, more so to those being of faith, because we become witnesses to our own spiritual destitute. Then our hearts began asking "when does it end?" If our vision of hope and faith is so perfect, why does it feel so hopeless?

As faith moves mountains, it also can create mountains, that way your hope and faith can be stirred up, and come back to you a little more perfect each time. God is the creator and author of perfect faith. If faith shows us the truth about sin and convicts us of our own sin, most reject that part of faith, they would rather wait on the faith they feel they deserve and understand. The truth is just faith produces fire that shakes and moves mountains! If by just faith love came down by love's own power and saving grace, then we would witness to a new found love instead of this "new found faith" or faith based faith.

Preachers love to preach on faith, yet they'll tell you in a heartbeat " let the God above take care of everything!" Above? Is that the faith they swear can move mountains?

Faith adheres to God who is inside of us. We became the body of Christ because faith understands the voice of the invisible God, who leads us to becoming His eyes, ears, mouth, hands, and feet, even putting His own heart in us! All so that we can serve in the world as the great men and women of the Bible did. Does your "faith" require you to look around for God? What are you looking around for? The Father, The Son, and The Holy Spirit are inside of you!

Or does your faith give you undeniable and measurable focus, that shows you who you are with God and without God? With purpose and without purpose? Where ever there is growth there is mercy. That's faith. How does faith dictate unmeasurable faith? The same as faith originates... under grace! Grace under fire in some circumstances. Faith rules where you reign, and mercy is faith's entourage. When Faith and courage become as one, hope lives. Hope lives beside faith's sworn attribution that " what goes up, must come down."

Hope is fraternal to faith " I'm all out of hope!" said no saint ever!

No matter how much courage one has, where there is no hope, faith cannot be measured. I told you faith is fair, and where there is no hope there is no provision. Hope is "pro - vision", you see the irony when you turn to faith and begin to see everything clearly and closely, because faith moves mountains...out of sight! With faith and hope side by side, you have manifesting grace. Faithful unto faithful, now those are words to live by!

Grace lives beside hope, hope lives beside faith, and faith lives by grace imputed unto you. His living vestibule!

A person who is truly justified by faith will have good works. If a believer has no good works, then he/she likely does not have the genuine faith in Christ.

For all that God has done for us, we are supposed to spend our lives paying Him back in fruit!

Matthew 7:15 " You will know them by their fruit."

Faith is not a rumor it's a ruler! The just shall live be faith; but what faith is accepted by God? In a very hypocritical and fake world, faith can also be just as manipulated. How is this possible? This "faith based faith" is without works and *"faith without works is dead faith" James 2:14 -26*. Works mean good fruit.

God gives to each of us who are called unto salvation a measure of faith. When that faith of a mustered seed becomes rhetorical unto God, then we are given another measure and grow our faith as such. Faith is internal power and rhetorical in Heaven. It is faith that judges belief. If faith wasn't important it wouldn't be tested so much! God accepted faith (just faith) can only be earned by faith, and death is earned by destitute faith (religious faith based faith)

Matt 7:22 -23" Many will say to me in that day, Lord, Lord, have we not prophesied in your name, and cast out demons in your name, and in thy name done many wonderful works? Then I will say to them plainly depart from me you workers of iniquity, **I NEVER KNEW YOU."**

WOW! The scariest four words you can ever hear in existence! We cannot just live by the "gift" of faith, we must live by the "power" of the gift of faith! Faith is the reason, but without power, faith is incomplete/ dead. Power = actions

Your faith should not stand in the wisdom of men, but in the power of God.

The Bible says The Word or message of the gospel itself is power!

Luke 4:32 "And they were astonished at his teaching, for his word was with power."

By the demonstration of the Spirit and of power, God still causes adulterers, prostitutes, fornicators, those in bondage to lust, rapists, pedophiles, homosexuals, murderers, thieves, liars, drug addicts, alcoholics, the depressed, and the psychopathic, to repent without ever consulting a Dr. or psychologist!

Acts 20:21 " Repentance toward God (Jehovah) and faith towards our Lord."(Jesus)

All by the power of the Word of God.

Romans 10:17

So I tell you "faith comes by hearing and hearing by the Word of God!"

Hebrews 4:2 " But the word preached did not profit them, not being mixed with faith in them that heard it."

2 Timothy 3:5 -7 " Having the form of godliness but denying the power thereof: from such people turn away!"

Believing Christ for the forgiveness of your sins will not save anyone if they do not repent! After all, even Satan and all his angels know that Jesus Christ is Lord, so do not believe in vain.

We cannot stop sin on our own, but by hearing the word, our measure of faith becomes rhetorical and manifests into power, His power! This power comes by faith to produce works of repentance, only then do we know we are of God.

1 John 3:6 " Whosoever abides in Him sinneth not: whosoever sinneth hath not seen him neither known him."

So many preachers are preaching forgiveness, but not preaching the power of God unto salvation.

Romans 1:16 "The power of the gospel is the power of God unto salvation."

If you are under the power of God, your under grace to be delivered.

Your either dead **to** sin, or dead **in** sin! So I ask you, are you satisfied with the faith you're operating in? Well? Is the Holy Spirit working in you to turn you away from your iniquities?

Acts 3:26

26 Unto you first God, having raised up his Son Jesus, sent him to bless you, in turning away every one of you from his iniquities

Scripture can hold all the faith you want it to, but it doesn't serve a purpose until you except that what you read there are exceptions, and those exceptions to all faith, are that faith without works is dead! Only God can save what is dead. Christ isn't dead, have you noticed? Not because of His spiritual faith alone, but by his obedience and surrender to God's will and not his own. Faith is bestowed to help us be made alive. Faith helps us discern, learn, understand, make manifest the truth, and surrender our will so God can take over. Faith makes it possible to do God's will. So why are people not benefiting when studying the Bible?

Hebrews 4:2

2 For unto us was the gospel preached, as well as unto them: but the word preached did not profit them, not being mixed with faith in them that heard it.

Hebrews 4:2 says they are not hearing the word of God mixed with faith. Faith is not believing God will do it all for you and give you everything you want. Faith is seeking what God wants.

Matthew 12:50

For whosoever shall do the will of my Father which is in heaven, the same is my brother, and sister, and mother.

So what does this all accomplish in us that faith alone does not? Listen closely, it's so that we shall become like our Lord and Savior, by living the word of God, as our Savior was also called **THE WORD!**

1 John 1:1 " In the beginning was the Word, and the Word was with God, and the Word was God."

Keep the faith that was bought by faith. Never surrender to faith based faith, which is faith in your own flesh. When faith doesn't deliver as expected, the problem is you.

The scriptures are as spiritual as it's Author, but to the prideful man who only cherry picks, and sugar coats, wanting his ears tickled to conform the gospel to his own lifestyle, then this man lives by his own putrid faith. We can't live by the mustered seed faith without growing, maturing, or producing fruit. The Lord warns us these trees will be uprooted and thrown into the fire! Faith has come along way from scripture where she started. Your faith has a beginning, middle, and end.

Faith is imperishable, but only where it is found. There is no Holy intrusion that will contradict your mustered seed faith, the only way the Holy Spirit is intruding on your faith (purposely) is by scripture. Faith is earned by justice. The statue of truth is that everything spoken in the word of God is truth, and faith assured you it was true, and hope made everything come alive by He that worketh by love. Also faith worketh by love.

Faith is the notion of the know how, and the power to prove anything without rhyme or reason; to sustain the know how physically. Now that's love!

For the human souls knowledge is not godly knowledge; yet the Holy Spirit is the producer of spiritual knowledge. "Aren't we all spiritual?" Afraid not. We are literally human and soul. There are not even any connectors by Satan. So what fuses a soul to spiritual things? Not Satan, not fallen angels, not even water baptism. **ONLY FAITH**.

Look around, have you ever wondered how faith moves mountains? Doesn't seem true does it? That's because it's a idiom. You are the mountain!

If I can move mountains by faith, then I can move anything by faith!

Earth doesn't move under Shiloh (state of rest) nor does it shake at the strong. The only way to move Heaven and Earth, is to become Heaven and Earth!

Trust Him and faith will council the spiritual countenance of just faith; but faith will never answer with out the blindfold on, which is faith's true witness and that's hope.

Faith worketh by love, love is incomplete without faith and hope, as Hope is incomplete without faith and love. Love hopes in all things, for this reason above all, love is the highest command, and if I have faith that can move mountains, but do not have love, I am nothing.

God didn't say perfect faith saves, he said you are saved by grace. That doesn't mean you don't have a serious decision to make. Faith is not sitting on Facebook all day witnessing that your saved by faith because that's what your preacher told you, and that you don't have to understand anything about the scripture because that's what preachers are for, or that as long as you have a good heart you are saved. The Bible says that the heart knows nothing of the spiritual things. Your heart is a deceiver in many ways, because your heart wants what your heart wants, contrary to how the Lord saves and what he considers worship. God's will is that faith comes by hearing the word, and that word will produce confidence, and that confidence will produce another measure of faith given by the Holy spirit; to produce solid food by the Holy Spirit!

That is God's will of the gift of dispensation, that you may hear all the Spirit is saying. If then the words of the Holy Spirit are cursed by your own omission, then cursed you will be by the words of the dispensation. So the decision is, do you believe in who you are carnally, or who God is spiritually? Most of us are to comfortable in our own being, instead of being stretched enough to fit into God's being. Jesus was so stretched by God, that he surrendered some of his being to truth, some to faith, some to courage, some to judgement, and some to true love, until he emptied all of himself of himself!(Ketosis). God chose you to be like his son, and Heaven chose you to be like her king. Too many people choose to be prisoners to this new found faith (faith based faith) of prosperity, grace, mercy, love, kindness, and sugar coated preachers that tickle their ears by cherry picking scripture, and they end up with other peoples scripts and experiences of God, and non of their own. Someone who is spoon fed by the world's views, cannot compare to one who seeks after God for themselves and knows the depths of how the Holy Spirit does speak, where the Lord lives, and can be found. We should be so full of God, that he only leaves us room to grow and breath. If you don't have much room for anyone else's teachings or experiences, then you know you found Him! So many people with this ordinary faith believe God's being and voice is only found in the Bible. God made a joke about this to me saying "oh by the way will you leave your Bible cracked so I can breath." LMBO! You won't necessarily find that sense of humor in the Bible, as God is more then the frame or book we place him in.

If The Bible is the Word, The Word is Christ, and Christ has risen to a higher ascension, then is he in or out? If God is omnipotent then how come people of ordinary faith believe he is not at liberty to transform, or conform to someone any way he chooses? Certainly they are not saying he is stuck in the Bible?

I have heard it all over the years, and my conclusion is this; common sense isn't common.

All in all we are reborn by faith and saved by grace.

Not all of us will be given the gift of extraordinary faith, or faith that would shape us all the same. **BORING**! We can see through out creation that's not how God works. All elephants are not Asian, and all monkeys are not Orangutans.

Just as the scriptures are forevermore, so is Christ's reign as King, but it didn't begin at the scriptures. Just as those Apostles speaking in the Bible weren't speaking as saints. Faith did not make them saints, God's grace did.

All in all, we are reborn by faith, and we are saved by grace.

Those who claim even the ordinary faith, must confess Christ by obeying a form of His own death, burial, and resurrection. In the same way we are not saved by faith only, but faith leads us to obedience or it simply is not faith.

1 John 5:4 "For whatsoever is born Of God overcometh the world: and this is the victory that overcometh the world, even our faith."

You can't expose knowledge until you have faith in it, or faith wouldn't exist faithfully.

Section Six

Hope

Romans 5:3 " We rejoice in our sufferings knowing suffering produces perseverance and perseverance character and character hope."

Hope is not something we obtain, because we've had it since a child. Hope showed her beautiful face all day when you were as innocent ones. Faith was not needed to see hope, because hope lives where hope lives. When you were a toddler you "knew" you couldn't die, am I right? Hope was your surety that when you dived off your parents furniture, some how you were going to have this magical landing! Hope is the surety that doesn't examine beforehand. The "ready, set, go!" Faith can move mountains, but hope is when you already know it's done. Ring around the Rosie; the kids know they are going to "all fall down" that's the reason they play and then spring back up again. Hope is also like the backseat of a car, it doesn't matter if it's junk or even rides, it's always there. Hope truly doesn't decrease, it's always fair, yet it is impressionable. Surely hope does not know who is or is not worthy. Hope balances everything. Hope is the gift worth rejoicing over and requiring your hand in God's over faith. So isn't it safe to say, since suffering produces perseverance, and perseverance character, and character hope, and hope produces faith, that neither suffering, nor perseverance, nor character, nor hope can truly be our sacrifices to God? Instead they are gifts from God! Since they are the substances that lead to the one thing that we must render to Him in love, in order to please Him and receive eternal life by His' grace. So is it not faith that is our sacrifice to God? Is faith not a sacrifice that we all should be examining ourselves for and humbly offer instead of patting ourselves on the back? We all have doubted God over petty things, even when He has showed us His faithfulness each Winter, Spring, Summer, and Fall. When someone puts more faith in the rhythm, rather then putting faith in the creator of the rhythm, I assure you God toils in his sacrifices.

We truly are not worthy of hope. Hope is a phenomenon, and is brave not hoping in herself or having to adhere to faith before she shows up. Hope is not a flower that blooms in the spring, but she's the seed that was planted by the planter for the flower in the spring. The seed is neither sure nor unsure that spring will come, or that she will even become a flower. She just lives where she lives.

Hope doesn't sit there "hoping" that someone will have faith that she will be a flower. Hope doesn't have to hope in herself because hope dances with hope alone. Hope is not a feeling or a reaction, so to speak. Yes hope can be produced, as in transpiring or brought forth by many things such as character, and that can bring hope out of someone; but hope has always existed within. Whether active or dormant. Hope is not a reaction, as if character is her spiritual and chemical compound. God is Hope! God is eternal and has always existed uncreated.

Faith sets in our understanding. Hope sets in our will. They differ in respects of office. (chambers of the Lord)

Faith -teaches, prescribes, and directs.

Hope - stirs up the mind that it may be strong, courageous, bold, that it may suffer and endure adversity, and patients for waiting on better things.

These two differ on touching their objects or special matter, where unto they look.

Faith's object has for "her" truth, to teach us to cleave to and look upon surly the Word and promise of things promised.

Hope has for "her" object, the goodness of God and looks upon good things even in the midst's of evil.

We judge with faith, yet God judges by our own hope and what our hope, hopes in. Figuratively speaking, hope and faith are our internal army, and does go hand in hand, yet God can separate, weed through, and read immensely.

2 Corinthians 1:12 " For our rejoicing is this the testimonies of our conscious that in simplicity and Godly sincerity, not with fleshly wisdom, but by the grace of God we have had our conversation in the world."

Hope lives, faith delivers. Hope delivers in struggle as her natures call, but the miracle happens when we believe. Hope is a exercise of faith (hope doesn't hope in hope, but holds hope for faith.) Hope is a departure from a loose lens of the here and now, or what the world sees about each other as having a Godly form and hoping that all people are good and created equal.

The heart wants what the heart wants. Therefore the hope a soul produces intentionally, is not reiterated as much by God, as faith is. For hope can be made morbid by a morbid world. As they put their hope in luck and evil rather then life.

That is why we wait on the righteous hope that is of God by faith, but not through faith, as they must stand together, because the righteousness of God is the only way to produce what is good and worthy in a man's hope and faith. If a man's faith is made up of his own substance and carnally motivated, how then would the same man produce righteous hope through such tainted faith, if one leads through the other? That is why this is a opposing opposition, because the substance of righteousness comes from God alone in each carefully weighed aspects of our lives.

Galatians 5:5

5For we through the spirit wait for the hope of righteousness by faith.

Hope is a ransom, not a physical tort! For their payment of sin was Christ!

So now that your vision or belief (hope) has risen to God's manifold, it is now his' ear to hear and his to judge. However glorious or evil, your hope now serves as an addendum, and heavenly host in exchange for your mouth. Trust God lives for you and not to count your sins. God lives to be faithful and true as promised, where you can't even be true to yourselves.

2 Timothy 2:13.13 If we believe not, yet he abideth faithful: he cannot deny himself.

The Samurai Sword

Hebrews 4 :12 " For the word of God is quick, and powerful, and sharper then any twoedged sword, piercing even to the dividing asunder of soul and spirit, and of the joints and marrow, and is a discerner of the thoughts and intents of the heart."

The Seven Spirits of God

1. Spirit of The Lord
2. Spirit of wisdom
3. Spirit of understanding
4. Spirit of counsel
5. Spirit of might
6. Spirit of knowledge
7. Spirit of The fear of the Lord

That is a lot of mystery! There is nothing the Lord cannot do. Think about a samurai sword. The samurai sword brings with him a wakizashi short sword and a tanto knife.

The wakizashi is the companion sword to the katana and together they are called daisho. These swords are series of layer after layer of forged stainless steel to give each blade an unparalleled level of strength and sharpness. There is no match! The samurai sword is long and lengthy, much to heavy to stand alone so there is a case called a sheath that carries the sword. Now the sheath will only show you just how long the sword is, but it will not show you the tenacity or velocity of the arm's might!

Paul identifies this sword as coming from the Holy Spirit(one of seven spirits of God). Adding that it is the word of God. The Holy Spirit is the source of the word.

2 Peter 1:20-21 " But know this first of all, that no prophecy of Scripture is a matter of ones own interpretation, for no prophecy was ever made by an act of human will, but men moved by the Holy spirit spoke from God."

John Wesley said " The Bible must have been written by God, or good men or bad men, or good angles or bad angels. But bad men and bad angels would not write it because it condemns bad men and bad angels. And good men and good angels would not deceive by lying about it's authority and claiming that God wrote it. And so the Bible must have been written - by God who by His Holy Spirit inspired men to record His words using the human instrument to communicate His truth."

Hebrews 11:3 " By faith we understand that the worlds were prepared by the word of God, so that what is seen was not made out of things which are visible."

Religion Vs. Relationship

Religion

What sorrow awaits you teacher of religious law.

Most religions today are a rip off and a dead pool. Their "worship" or religion is "tit for tit", as they want rewarded for everything they do, and multiple teachings of prosperity, everything is " prosper prosper prosper!" The only ones who are receiving, are the preachers and deacons. Those are handouts not blessings!

So then what are the congregations suppose to think when they don't get that blessing in which they sowed a 200.00 seed for?

"Oops maybe God ran out?" Many of these religions don't carry the fire of The Holy Spirit, or preach sound doctrine. God doesn't need a single thing from humans. Not worship, praise, good works, and certainly not our money! God is **NOT** broke have you noticed? Those who deeply know The

Lord, will deeply know His suffering. People don't like pain, so they are afraid to find God, who wrote the book on pain! He never said it should be easy. He said it would be worth it!

The Word of God tells us it IS a painful, cursed world, and a real personal relationship with your Savior is the only way. Instead most people choose to believe that a preacher who just stands there week after week, as if he is the answer, or holds all the answers by the power of The Holy Spirit. Yet when you leave church your still limping, broken down with a bad hip, and can't even stand up to worship over a bad knee. What are you limping for? The real question is what are you living for? Where is the power and proof of your relationship with Christ, The Healer, The Deliverer, Yolk Breaker, and He who strengthens?

Literally how is your "walk" or "stand" honoring The Almighty when your full of infirmities, that your beloved preacher or elders can't cast out because they have **NO** power? They focus on prophecy, but it's actually "im-prophecy" improper - prophecy! Not only is it a embarrassment for God and hard to bear, but it's an embarrassment on every head that participates in this derision and parody.

You might as well pull the white sheet over your head, because they are not teaching the Word of God, as they are suppose to be a witness to what they preach. Instead they're full of their own self righteousness and self power. God help them, they need to repent! Maybe if the congregation would repent, they wouldn't need these fake "healers" pushing people down faking God's divine healing. The Earth herself has never needed man to heal throughout history. Is that the "healers" way of saying God only speaks through sign language? God's Spirit ministers faithfully to his people. Their isn't a preacher alive that doesn't want to move in all the gifts of the Holy Spirit, but you cannot just help yourself!

The Spirit gives unto each as He wills.

1 Corinthians 12:18 But in fact, God has arranged the members of the body, every one of them, according to His design.

Matthew 6:33 33 But seek ye first the kingdom of God, and his righteousness; and all these things shall be added unto you.

We are called to receive The Word, minister the Truth, and everything else will be added unto us. Without a relationship with the Holy Spirit, the Bible is boring, convicting, and made of no understanding, without wisdom or knowledge to the one who relies on his own understanding. **NO** spiritual eye = **No** gain.

When Christ gave his life, men gave up and kissed their own pastors, who bore them to death, literally! Many are amongst those who don't teach "Repent or Parish" as Jesus taught, because repentance is something they are unsure of, so they won't test the waters, being among sharks, they would rather tarry on prosperity and self righteous equality, then move forward by the will of God, understanding men cannot live by bread alone, but by the very word of God, which is proof that men must seek first the kingdom of God, then everything else will be added to the true seekers. Where is the love outside their own outline and routine? Certainly if a preacher is lead by God, the congregation would also be led, instead of being full of worry over what imaginary lines would be crossed if someone gets offended. (God forbid!) We are told not to worry about what we will say because when given the opportunity to speak on behalf of God's people and of even God himself, we will be given the accuracy and wisdom that the scripture holds, by the power of the Word himself! There is such miracle as revelatory preaching by the Holy Spirit, and then you have what is considered "learned" preaching. Many religious doctrine preaching's are so rehearsed, that you would have thought each person reciting these scriptures where a true spokes person for the gospel of our Savior, but mistakenly that's just acting and learned behavior, as the desire may be there but the fire of the acquitted is rare. It's about time they file a motion for "appeal" because as the Word has it, the Word always wins in God's favor! The fire of God is instantaneous, and belongs with those as a ramification of true speakers testifying **WITH** the Lord, not to those speaking openly, carrying on freely about the scriptural moments God's chosen and anointed ones spoke fervently about the rest that would follow, and speak producing the same fire, that many would be slain by from the Lord. Perhaps there's no trust. You cannot lead if you aren't led, as you can't spread the fire if you have none to spread!

Hebrews 1:7

7 And of the angels He says:
"Who makes His angels spirits
And His ministers a flame of fire

All preachers and elders need to examine their selves and wash their hands, especially when the head of the church and church leaders are witnessing about God's healing, but being dealt with by God in a whole different fashion. To witness of healing, you must be a witness to healing, or else you can't preach about something you don't know. Giving false hope because your not sure you have hope in it. You can't give what you don't have, just as I said you can't spread the fire if you have not, and you won't pass the hope if you seek not. All that we need to be productive in Christ, in the body, and as an assembly is there for the grasping as long as it is assembled together with great reform by Christ!

"Obey and Lay" not "cheat and retreat" Laying on of hands is a serious reflection! So isn't it safe to ask, where is the spiritual reflection? You know the one God gives when you bow to him instead of bowing to your neighbor and pastor? That's why the congregations have become a reflection of their pastoral hazing. As he speaks they speak, what he doesn't say neither will they, and what is untaught will remain unlearned.

Relationship

What if Adam and Eve would have called on the Lord for guidance, who was not only their God and Creator, but their friend? It would have changed their life as well as humanity.

Proverbs 9:10 " The fear of the Lord is the beginning of wisdom: and the knowledge of the holy is understanding."

1 John 2:23 " He who confesses the Son has the Father also."

There is no doubt if we want a relationship with The Alpha and Omega, The Great Elohim, and omnipotent Father God, we must go through His only begotten Son.

In order to take advantage of this magnificent and unfathomable promise, we must turn to the Word of God with all humility, to earnestly seek his Son, in **ALL** His entirety! Don't let other people write your scripts and ideas about God. That just wont do. Our Lord is our personal Savior. We must take personal, very personal, what He does for us individually, and what wrath He saves us from when we rely on Him for our salvation. If you were the only one in need of rescuing, my friend Jesus Yeshua Messiah, would have died for you alone in His Father's wrath. What a friend we have to share!

John 15:13 "For no greater love hath no man then this, that a man lay down His life for his friends."

Not only did He suffer, struggle on the cross, and die, but He also **lived** for us!

No greater love then the Father to give His only begotten son, to be slain in His own wrath for the transgressions of the whole world.

Jeremiah 29:11 "surely I know the plans I have for you says the Lord, plans for your welfare and not to harm, to give you a future with hope."

The Lord desires us to be His and to really know Him, not because we are worthy or deserving, but because **HE IS**! Have you ever asked God "why me? or "why was I even born?" Have you felt unworthy of your calling or gifts? Even unworthy to share the gospel, because well maybe your just not living up to it? Your not alone, but if we knew all that Christ suffered, we should surely feel deep conviction!

As I was in months of fellowship with God in all his entirety, my gifts and anointing was increased.

1 Corinthians 3:7 "neither he who plants nor he who waters is anything, but God who gives the increase."

During diligent worship, prayer, and sitting at God's feet and seeking his face, he began speaking to me audibly saying;

"Katie, I gave my life so you could find yours. I fulfilled your scriptures, all of them. I AM The Lord. I Am the love of your life. Patiently believe in Me.

*I was left hanging on a cross, shedding blood on holy ground. Now come and face Me. You have no idea the price put on just one of you. Stripped of My innocence so you can have yours. Refunds are **NOT** an option. Blasphemed and ridiculed as they whipped My flesh off "so your the Son of God huh?" They threw stones as the liars masqueraded around trying and testing Me. God My Father would not help Me for it was not My will, but My Fathers allocated will. Whipped in judgement for every sin known to man. For every sin that entered into ones' conscious. Bought by Yeshua Hamashiach. You want to talk about conviction?*

I don't think you do. No man born or has died, knows the conviction of the Holy Spirit that was placed on Me! No one knows the judgment that was received by the Son of man. I have a job to do. I died for all the sins committed of humanity and resurrected. God changed My life forever! I am a very rich and respected man, who came down to deliver you. God restored Me as His only Son, glory hallelujah! You are soul of My soul, body of My body, blood bought bones of My bones. Come now and face Me! I have stuck My life on a serious crossed line. (The Cross) Innocent and honest. I never denied you life abundantly, abounded in Me.

Son of man was lowered lower then you. No man is deserving or worthy of anything, especially the Light, yet God gives it to us in handfuls. There is no fear in love, trust Him. I called you. Surly I knew you before you were ever created."(Jeremiah 1:5) Thus says the Lord.

Worship Worship Worship

Isaiah 61:7 " instead of shame you shall have double honor, and instead of confusion they shall rejoice in their portion."

Responsibility is not just a birthright, or a model person, its a great helper.

Words of wisdom, *Matthew 6:33 "Seek ye first the Kingdom of God and everything else will be added unto you."*

Confessing and turning back in ruff times, improves the worship and the relationship with God. It's not about what we have done that He is truly concerned with (all fall short of the glory of God) but what we do about it!

1 Peter 4:8 Love covers a multitude of sins.

Worship holds no water unless The Great Elohim Himself can sing about it!

Most believers today are missing the soul purpose of worshipping in Spirit and in Truth. Worship is for us to join with God, not God to join with us. If we want God to hold the service, then we must let God lead the service! Isn't that diversity? Isn't it? Tell me who holds the map? Who knows where God is, or can find him right where he's at? (please don't speak all at once) Or who washes away sins during faithful worship? I'll tell you why their singing, because there is money involved. The truth is not found in worship as most people think it is. That's only the beginning of truth unto who God decides to put truth in.

John 14:6 " I am the Way, the Truth, and the Light."

We must let God lead the way, words are just words that are becoming meaningless because it's all for "velour." (imitation fabric resembling velvet) example (not a physical demonstration.) Princes wear velvet, evidently, so why are most secular worshippers covering themselves with plush imitation velvet robes as they do? God didn't give us the invitation to preform a imitation worship service! God is undeniable! Richly clothed in restitution, and He specifically, characteristically, demands the acknowledging that He surly is who everybody says, and sings that He is!

Praise is not always worship! Worship only happens when your heart and soul make way for God, it's for those who know Him, and a invitation for those who don't know him, but want to. Not the other way around! Worship is not an invitation for God to know you. If God doesn't know you, its because you haven't acknowledged him in honesty and truth. **NOT** your truth, and if your not sure which is different then don't speak! Be still there is a way to seek God. Be still and know that God is still who he says he is...Love; and he is always where he is!

Boy who would have ever thought it? We need to introduce God to these tired congregations who want to know who God is, but don't want to face him. "Deliver me!" is their favorite confession, and prosperity their favorite expectation. Shameful! Vexed cold! That certainly is a bold request by a congregation who hasn't even found, let alone known God. The truth is most everyone is ignorant when it comes to worship, faithfulness, faith, responsibilities, true confessions, repentance, and the list goes on and on! Singing is not for God's purpose, worship is. "Oh but singing is worship!" they exclaim. (Need I say More?) Their singing is their worship, and it's to cover them with their own velour as I stated. I'm a visual person, so God shows me things through analogies. This might make you feel skeptical because I use the word medicine, but as I said it's just an analogy.

Worship is like medicine. You cannot take a healthy dose if your taking it every few minutes, your only hurting yourself. You cannot skip regular doses here and there and just double up (or do over time) when ever you feel. You defiantly cannot substitute with "medicine" your not use to. Just as you can't worship only when your heart is sick, you will never find Him that way, because like medicine, it's hard to find the right medication and dosage for all the time that has lapsed while you were without. God didn't sacrifice for that "prescription," or "dosage!"

I'm sorry if the truth hurts, but it's time we learn the hard way, by opening our eyes. Is that to much to ask? God asked me one day, He said *" If I am such a safe haven, then why is every person a liar?"* and He demanded a answer by saying *"answer quickly!"* I gave Him my best answer as the scriptures say in *Romans 3:4 All men are liars and only God is the truth.*

Psalm 116:11

11 I said in my haste, All men are liars.

God replied to me with disappointment;

"Listen closely. Search Me. There is a lot more then human worship. There is spiritual worship, and who knows what spiritual worship is, and is not?

Let Me start by saying it is not human worship. Who knows what human worship is, and is not? Answer quickly. For why am I still wasting time simplifying everything if you truly know who God is? Evidently God is a reflection of human worship. Katie if that were the case, human worship is an embarrassment to a King who listens faithfully. Human worship should be labeled **BANISHED NOT FOR CONSUMPTION OF ANY LIFE FORM!** *As a serious* **WARNING** *label."* said the Lord.

HUMAN WORSHIP = persons who worship with their own understanding and without help (simplify) .

"This is the reason I come, as your teacher not your pleaser, God's pleaser." said The Holy Spirit.

"Discern the light or discern the lie? Discern the way or discern the truth? All the above Katie. If you have the light then you have the eyes, the quickening, and the washing of regeneration. All glory, power, knowledge, praises, and honor to Him who holds it all.

I sent My Holy spirit as affirmation at Pentecost(Acts 2:1-13) .

I sent My Holy Spirit for regeneration at the Cross.

I sent My Holy Spirit for Salvation, when did I disclose regulations?

I sent My Holy Spirit to the grave for resurrection.

I sent My Holy Spirit on the Sabbath for confirmation.

Did I not prophesy in Isaiah without regards to how it makes you feel?

Did I not prophesy in the book of Daniel how responsible I am to a just man?

Well, did I not? Did I not consecrate My Holy Spirit to Shadrach, Meshach, and Abednego? Or In the book of Lamentations, did I not feel bad for that desolate wicked city Zion? Or was she left desolate to the end of the earth? Well then? Well then! Why does it hurt so bad to Jehovah Hatov? The greatest survival the world has ever seen and prophesies over and over and over, why does it not look so amazingly exemplified? The Holy spirit wants what He wants. Where are the blessings that you all talk of? Where are the Royal Blessings? Don't you know? Where is the excitement of a new life as a new creation? I do not see it in worship on any stage! I guess you have to do a lot of thinking to be in ministry, because worldly confidence is overwhelming to My soul, who's worship is in Spirit and Truth. How's that for Amazing grace? I'll tell you what the world needs, they need some auto tune desperately! They cannot sing His amazing graces by 10,000,000 microphones! They could not contain them! Do you know what they say? What everyone says! Hardly what God says. Do you want to know what a true worshipper says? Not Figaro, Figaro, Figaro (magnify the Galileans)

Katie a true worshipper does not need to speak a single word.

His voice is in His cries. Your voice is not only skin deep, your voice is Holy worship. So then how does a voice get so ran over by the same worship/praise songs over and over and over? The same way it ran away over and over and over. Without My Spiritual Helper a lot of My perfect things get ran over. Why do you think that is? It's because My Spiritual Helper is My Prophet and beloved Prophecy. How did you know the Holy Spirit was not a Prophet? Did you listen carefully to the Holy Scriptures that ordained Him a Prophet? Intercessor? A Holy Mediator? "So what do you want from Me?"(replied the Holy Spirit). "A Bible lesson? I tried to, but you fell asleep as soon as I started speaking. Well I must of bored you. Someone has to do it, and it will not be a prisoner of the worldly assembly. So I ask you what do you want from me, if your right all the time and faith can move mountains, but it cannot obtain a imperative worship? Ye good and selfish. It is time to repent of worldly lullabies. It is making them sleepy and boy is it to early for worshippers to be sleeping! Soul be quieter! Listen as an adoration to the Holy Spirit. Yet no Helper is heard, because their aim is spiritual salutations, that is not honorable. No penitence. No solitude. It's all about what I can give them freely. Did I not give them enough from my own hand? Did I prophesy over them in truth and in spirit then walk away? No. Thank Him if you know Him!" Thus says The Holy Spirit of God.

So know I ask why does it have to be so difficult for the Lord to be the hero of the Scriptures? Not only did He slay the villains, but He won the battle, ALL our battles! People act as if The Victor who has already won, is still fighting somebody's cancer, pneumonia, or herpes. Christ will **NEVER** have to fight those Appalachians ever! As He already did it! Christ consummated mankind's survival.

John 16:33 " These things I have spoken unto you, that in me ye might have peace. In the world ye shall have tribulation: but be of good cheer; I have overcome the world."

The Lord spoke to me saying;

"Katie, I commiserate on The Judgement Seat for humankind's redemption over and over and over. I grieve all day long, if a day was as long in human years as it is light years away. I grieve over creation and My Holy Spirit that My people do not deserve or verify as Holy, Holy, Holy unto Me. My people are banishing My true Holy scriptures for their Compassion's and worldly passions. You cannot exchange My Compassion's and

passions over worldly people! That equals judgement! Drudgery equals no Compassion's or works that fan the flame.

Am I the Great Elohim or some kind of super attendant to all of you?

Where is My honor? Where is My recompense? Where is the fire that I save with? Is it all up to you to bring the fire and recompense, that I save with?

Well if you got it, then take your hands off of it!

I am the Great Elohim that breathes with fire, should I hold my breath just to please you? Afraid not! I have been worshipped by my own breath of fire and smoke all on my own, now tell me is it worth it? Is it worth it to worship by His honor, by His Holy Spirit? Yes? Or yes? Then why will you not simmer down and stop blowing smoke and mirrors. There is only room for one of those imitators, and it is not here! Do not let the rapture let you down, so to speak. Focus on The Marriage." Thus saith the Lord.

Spiritual VS Sensual;

1 Corinthians 2:14 " But the natural man does not receive the things of the Spirit of God, for they are foolishness to him; nor can he know them, because they are spiritually discerned."

1 John 4: 24 " God is Spirit and those who worship Him must worship in spirit and in truth."

James 4:10 " Humble yourselves in the sight of the Lord and He will lift you up."

Worship is not just worship, as it is measured by faith. As a gift from the Lord.

We don't have to worship, we **GET** to worship! Worship is very scriptural. Worship is rhetorical. When we worship God how he desires us to, without being loud and proud, or chauvinistic like it's time to kick off our shoes and have a dance off, then he always gives back to us, as we are one in the same with his Holy Spirit! Everyone wins and as the Word says in *1 Corinthians 13:8 love never fails.* God definitely has a say in how we worship Him. After all He knows what He likes, and is it not for Him? Then why must He share His Holy stage with those who make worship about their own pride, and think worship is for vision and a dispensary of gifts?

Psalms 46:10 Be still and know that I am God.

This refers to the ceasing of strife, while singing slowly and quietly. Praise and worship should be God centered. There is a preoccupation with God, not with excitement, enthusiasm, or self energizing. We are not encouraged to "get high" or all excited, but be humble. For the Father is seeking such to worship Him.

John 4:23 " But the hour cometh, and now is, when true worshippers shall worship the Father in spirit and in truth: for the Father is seeking such as his worshippers."

Psalms 95:6 " O come, let us worship and bow down: let us kneel before the LORD our maker."

Romans 14:11 "For it is written, As I live saith the Lord, every knee shall bow to me, and every tongue shall confess to God."

For who knows how the Lord's heart does produce fire? Or how to fan the flames? The Lord our God is never boring, so be creative in worship. Praise can be worship, but it doesn't end there.

Colossians 3:23 "And whatsoever ye do, do it heartily, as to the Lord, and not unto men."

The Lord is very musically inclined, we just have to examine our music if we are a true responsible worshipper. It's always good to ask God what he prefers. I'm sure He doesn't want the same thing all the time! God doesn't want pattern, he wants mind over matter. When much is given much is expected.

Forgiveness

1 John 1-19 If we confess our sins and ask for forgiveness He is faithful and righteous to forgive us our sins.

Matthew 6-15 If we forgive others our Father in Heaven will forgive us our trespasses.

Do you know that worrying is a sin? Its unconstitutional in Christ's courts. We don't always know we are worrying, but it can be helped. No matter who we are or what we have done, He is risen and we have a good faithful Lord who loves us just as we are, and just as we were.

Romans 8:38 "For I am persuaded that neither death nor life neither angles nor demons neither past nor future nor any powers neither high nor depth nor anything else in creation shall be able to separate us from the love of God which is in Christ Jesus our Lord."

Forgiveness is worship with clean unstained hands. There is no transgressions that our Lord and our Father cannot forgive. Neither big nor small. Sin is sin.

It's not the matter of the degree of sin, but what you don't say or feel about your iniquity is your shame. Pride persuades you that everybody sins just in different ways. Pride will tell us God expects us to sin. Well that's only partly true. The Word says *"Be Holy for I am Holy" 1 Peter 1:16*. That means stomping out your transgressions with The Holy Spirit who is your helper. If you believe in a holy life style, you can achieve it, and surrender is what moves him by our hope in his grace. As to the same with faith, live by faith not by sight. The just will be forgiven for the just live by faith.

Hebrews 10:38 For the just shall live by faith: but if any man draw back my soul shall have no pleasure in him.

He is a rewarder of just faith. Having faith that He is faithful to always forgive all unintentional sins and most intentional sins, if we seek His face and turn away from our iniquity. I am convinced there is no sin greater then another that He cannot forgive. That is **NOT** to say all sins are the same. Sins are categorized as follows, intentional or premeditated sins, unintentional sins, graven sins (sin that leads to death) or abominations, and blasphemies. Sin is sin whatever shape or degree, and *"the wages of all sin is death." Romans 6:23.*

We must remember God is Holy, Holy, Holy, even when his eyes are beholding all good and evil. Proverbs 15:30. Forgiveness is a free gift, as is salvation. All God's gifts are free to us because Christ paid the ultimate price and made the ultimate sacrifice! Forgiveness did **NOT** come cheap, that is why He is dedicated to it! *Ask and you shall receive. (James 4:3)* Don't be to busy to *seek God while He can still be found and forgiveness can still be received. (Isaiah 55:6).* I don't believe you always have to seek Him to obtain forgiveness, He is faithful to who He is. It's His nature.

2 Timothy 2:13 If we are faithless He remains faithful for He can not deny who He is.

Faithful to the faithless? Now that is gracious! Strength comes and goes but forgiveness surrounds the Mercy Seat. He who sits on the Mercy Seat is longsuffering, faithful, full of compassion and mercy. Gracious is the Lord! Gracious is the Father Jehovah, who graces us with his presence through mercy, and the Savior is a splitting image of His greatness! Greatness isn't all about being great, but the ability to be meek, containing all that power with humility. It's not about being superior and full of power, but power to crush Satan and sins of humanity one confession at a time. The Accuser loves to accuse all of mankind and confuse us with fake love, the kind that turns a blind eye when we sin. Sweeping it under the rug is the world's definition of love and forgiveness. Well that's not humility that's pride! That is why the curtain or veil to the spiritual is so special, because His Holy Spirit is our mediator who doesn't sleep day or night, and knows all our sins and emotions, even what we should pray for. He is the one you should thank. He is your courage to ask Jehovah Father to forgive a person other then yourself or to help you be forgiven by someone else. The Holy Spirit has His hand in all of that! Do not be unsightly, forgiveness isn't all about shame, for God to draw a crowd, or condemn you by sin. People use the words condemn and convict as words to shame you or shame sin. In actuality, it's not to curse you, as sin already is the curse, and the damage has already been done. Forgiveness is actually a spiritual license to convict one's way of living or well rehearsed story. You see stories change but God never does. Forgiveness convicts someone into change, to live without the rehearsals and drama queens, and to depict a new and better way of living above the sinning, not necessarily without it.

Luke 7:47 Therefore I say to you, her sins, which are many, are forgiven, for she loved much. But to whom little is forgiven, the same loves little."

Conviction can count as brotherly love. As a way to lift the burdens of the world off your shoulders, and as weighing in your spirit how detrimental society's spin on fun and love can be if we initiate or be the bigger person in forgiveness. We all have a past and a job. Not to live under a "one world order" or be regressive. You tell me what's being accomplished within the human race to continue the first and final Commands? It's a lonely world. No one truly loves anymore, or practices survival. It's all about fancy expensive things, money, internet, social media, a million selfies, and competitive physiques striving to be perfect. Isn't it sad that children are literally human clones of society, and they don't need or seek God?

They have no need for truth. Parents don't raise them to scratch their heads or raise a brow at what God is doing as they are suppose to. It baffles God how dumb a person can truly be.

Hosea 4:6,

6My people are destroyed for lack of knowledge. Because you have rejected knowledge, I also will reject you from being My priest. Since you have forgotten the law of your God, I also will forget your children. 7The more they multiplied, the more they sinned against Me; I will change their glory into shame

Job 36:11-12

11"If they hear and serve Him, They will end their days in prosperity And their years in pleasures. 12"But if they do not hear, they shall perish by the sword And they will die without knowledge.

Everyone is entitled of their own opinion, but excuse me, when did God rule the world with Facebook, internet, computer inventions, or the latest game and toy?

From Genesis to current day, God managed to become a human, A King, save humanity, obtain the keys to death and Hades, send a third person The Helper, (so you could look yourself in the mirror and not completely hate who is starring back at you) gave you the option to choose true love, and someone you could call your best friend, and truly trust. Non of it's good enough! Its unreal how unreal people truly are. No one wants to feel, well how do you expect to worship a Savior who's life cannot be bought and who's light you cannot see? It's horrible. So what I'm saying is, what is your definition of true love? Game councils or Facebook?

Power is powerful and God is not going to change to win someone over.

I change not says the Lord of Hosts. *(Malachi 3:6)* Is He ice cream? Hard when it's cold and soft when it's hot? Afraid not. Difference is, He always manifests to who ever comes to find him and always will. The God of Heaven and Earth has many mysteries that he would love to expose, if someone would be romantic, and truly trust Him for all the answers humans would ever, ever need. Someone brave enough to seek Him and know His heart. It's not about what you've done, it only matters what you do. Our journeys are epic, you will never have this same chance to know Him in the same way if you don't trust Him, honor Him with true faith, and stay in the hope to have vision even through the nightmares. Last but not least, seek Him, always seek Him.

The Rubik's Cube

People know that the Rubik's cubes is achievable, and can even be mastered in one's own mind. Regardless of the endless possibilities of movement, there's only one accomplishment; solve the Rubik's cube. Then you start over, twisting and turning in order to get the same results. No matter how much you twist and turn, or even push it aside from time to time, it's never finished until it's finished.

If you keep messing up, you may decide to try again later, and there it sits, the same as you left it. It doesn't change. Any way you turn the cube it teaches you another lesson. Whether right side up or upside down, or columns left to right. The only one who can determine what's up, down, left, or right, is the eye of the beholder. When it gets to hard you may pass it around, looking for someone to take you as far as they can to obtain your accomplishment, only to find that when it's handed back to you, you can't find the same pattern of reasoning, so your just as messed up as you started. Just as unfinished.

To say that God is like a Rubik's cube is a far cry, but the moral of this analogy is, all the help from friends and family just can't cut it when the Lord is one in the same, regardless of trial and error, or mountains of prosperity. Same mountain, different climbers. Rushing in to anything can only make it worse, as each move or turn has to be strategically planned, with hope for the other sides. No matter the faith that your playing with; big or small, there's only one of many outcomes that faith controls, and that's reason. The reason to play and the reason to start over.

It's a no brainer, God is more then a brain tease. Unlike the Rubik's cube, God's unique design is to help and guide, no matter who the world says He is, or regardless of the course to achieve. Fact of the matter is, longsuffering and longevity are important in accessing God. Faith is not the reason you wake up each morning God is. No matter how much faith you have or the type of faith you operate in, faith does not change who God is or his countless ways. Faith doesn't come by who we expect God to be. The story doesn't change the writer, just as faith is not based off of the way one flies, in retrospect; it's the reason one **DOES** fly!

Section Twelve

Everything Is Everything

Ecclesiastes 3" To everything there is a season, and a time to every purpose under the heaven."

Everything is everything to anyone who needs anything. Christ's life is not all about pleasing you and yours. The Holy spirit is our helper, but your weight you will carry, each carries his own weight as it is his/her story. People try to go around things in life, but God does not go around things, for he lives through them. If you are trying to get God to go around something, why not take him around your family and friends, where he belongs? Yet people make it into a burden to minister, or witness to family and friends, as if God's weight is a burden.

Matthew 11:30 "for my yolk is easy and my burden is light."

These are his weak people with weak souls. No matter how weak, weak is weak, right? Here's a conundrum; the strong isn't always for the weak of all sizes, because the strong cannot be made weak easily, but weak can be made strong

64

quickly, for it is already granted to those who hold it! Do you know what it is?

It's **RECOMPENSE!** That's why it's not all about our lives, as much as it is about Jesus, and what he has already done for our lives! You're not always to run in a race/marathon that doesn't compete. So whether you run or walk, will you not complete the calling in which you came? Either to help or be helped? We the people do not make humans like we use to! There's no sincerity, and no sense of right and wrong. People are made weak unto suicide over relationships, and there is no separation between their confidence and pride because it all runs together in arrogance! Where is the recompense God is entitled to? Love is a battlefield not a prison. God has never turned his back on a friend, yet humanity is a back turner. Jesus turned his life over so humanity could finally see that God is not a God who only wants worship. Didn't the Lord tear the temple down because of beautiful liars and religious fakes? I guess it didn't get everyone's attention in showing that your offerings are not good enough. Not then not now. God is constantly grieving because he has lost man in his love. God offered his own son, and you are to be saved by his love, by his life, and by his death. Yet everyone declares to everyone "your saved, your saved." He's not at your wishes command. People think because they choose Him, that they can choose His love according to what they want it to look, sound, and feel like. No one has the power to fathom God's love, so for that reason, before you commit your life to him, you better love him.

Recompense to the Lord can come in many forms, and one of them is exposing imposters. They are the ones who return with oil in their lamp stands or half of their candles' wick, which means they're not sharing their light. The wax around a candle determines who's been lighting who's wick, and the wick will never burn as brightly when it has been sitting in a puddle of its own wax, only when it's turned as if lighting someone else's wick. If God has to hold up his "magnifying glass" to see your wick, then your more then a conqueror in Christ! People don't practice what they preach, instead they brag but don't reach. Some believers will not share the gospel, even though Christ has commanded his followers to do so, because it would make them a hypocrite as they are still living in sin. No one should ever stop sharing the gospel because they are still a prisoner to sin, but they should repent so they are no longer hypocrites. Then the Lord gets double the glory, because they are sharing the gospel, and they are a witness to spiritual transformation. That's recompense!

There is no one who has ever been through your life, and most are perfect strangers to the battlefield of God's love, but the love you find there, has never been explained the same twice. We may never find God's love for a man exactly the same as the last man that witnessed his love. God's love wills and it won't it does and it don't.

The Lord constantly tells me *"everything is everything*!" So worship is everything, and everything can be worship! It doesn't stop at praise, it's showing up, giving devotion, recompense, adoration, fellowship, ministry, obedience, repentance, and surrender. It's not about where you worship, or who your in front of, because they don't know your past, God knows where you've been and how far you've come. God is everything to anyone who needs anything.

Section Thirteen

Fighting Fire With Fire

Deuteronomy 4:2 "For the LORD your God is a consuming fire, a jealous God."

Matthew 3:11-12 11 I indeed baptize you with water unto repentance. but he that cometh after me is mightier than I, whose shoes I am not worthy to bear: he shall baptize you with the Holy Ghost, and with fire:

12 Whose fan is in his hand, and he will thoroughly purge his floor, and gather his wheat into the garner; but he will burn up the chaff with unquenchable fire

Numbers 31:23 Everything that can endure the fire, you shall make it go through the fire, and it shall be clean: nevertheless it shall be purified with the water of purification: and all that cannot endure the fire you shall make go through the water.

You don't fight fire with love, that's a mistake evidently. It's smolder or be smoldered, or as the saying goes kill or be killed. In this case, I'm referring to their flames they are burning in, over ungodly desires and lusts, they must be put out! If we neglect to spiritually discern by being weak, we can either be consumed by the weaknesses of the ungodly, or if we are careless and light the wrong wick in the wrong order (as some candles have several wicks) we run the risk of getting 3rd degree burns as fire spreads quickly! Nobody wants an itty-bitty flame regardless of what it comes from, so then we run a risk of fanning the wrong kind of fire that won't produce love, that only produces conviction to the ungodly and fans it toward the elusive as smoke to their own eyes. It's risky business to go into the fire to snatch some one out who is on the wrong side of the flames. Love is a battlefield but it's not a prison, and sometimes love doesn't always look like love to someone who isn't in love. Sometimes love doesn't always look the same from up above as it does to us down here. The Lord said there is no fear in love, but yet a lot of us down here are afraid of losing someone they love and they let love be their prison instead of their peace and solitude. It's true love isn't what it use to be, when a man would lay down his life for his friends with no shame, whether they were wrong or right, whether they were hurt or the one doing the hurting. And it's true that the truth isn't the truth anymore it's a mantra, and the fire is something in Revelations that everyone is scared of and not what they're here living for! That same fire is the reason that there is no fear in true love; now isn't that ironic? Yes love is a battle zone, but because of that same fire, we don't ever have to be afraid or prisoners because that love is what produces the fire that separates us from the ones that the Lord will separate us away from. This fire that I am produced from and fed from, is what I have become a witness to, by being formed from. I am an estate from which power and honor resonates by His Holy manifold to operate in the supernatural, not to impress men but to impress Him. This fire is omnipresent and consumes where ever it divides.

You can run to the Great Constable of Love, or run from The Great Divisionary, but you'll never go far because He is who he says He is, and no man can hide from a Consuming Fire!

Section Fourteen

The Truth Transforms

Psalm 86:11 Teach me your way, O LORD, that I may walk in your truth; unite my heart to fear your name.

We cannot defend the Word until we are molded, motivated, and merged by the Word of God. There is no cheap way to understand the Bible. Psalms 119 gives us a number of statements about the word of God.

Psalm 119:89 (a) Because no one should esteem God's word according to the changes of things in this world, he shows that it abides in heaven, and therefore is immutable.

"What is truth?" asked Pilate. Jesus answered "thy word is truth."

God didn't breath into the scripture, but breathed the scriptures out, and chosen men held the pen of God.

Romans 3:4 God forbid: yea, let God be true, but every man a liar; as it is written, that thou mightest be justified in thy sayings, and mightest overcome when thou art judged.

God forbid every man be a liar, as a liar cannot be helped, because when he speaks he speaks of his own character, and the countenance of his soul witnesses against him as the book of John says;

John 8:44 44You belong to your father, the devil, and you want to carry out his desires. He was a murderer from the beginning, refusing to uphold the truth, because there is no truth in him. When he lies, he speaks his native language, because he is a liar and the father of lies. 45But because I speak the truth, you do not believe Me.

In the book of *Mosiah 4:12 he says "we shall grow in the knowledge of the glory of Him who created us."* What is knowledge? Power! Power such as to repent of sin, it's obtained little by little and bit by bit, so that we will be humbled and grateful when a single sin is repented of. This transformation is not a group transformation. The Holy Spirit is your personal helper, and indeed your personal transformation is very critical to the Body of Christ, as it produces great ramifications! Just as if the head is sick the whole body grows sick and the heart grows faint because the body hears everything the mind says.

Isaiah 1:5

5Where will you be stricken again, As you continue in your rebellion? The whole head is sick And the whole heart is faint. 6From the sole of the foot even to the head There is nothing sound in it;

Jesus said in John 14:6 I am the way, the truth, and the life: no man cometh unto the Father, but by me.

Now God spoke to me months before writing this book and He said with concern;

"To many people are focused on pinpointing the time of judgement and Christ's return, which is only slowing the process of every single person for certain. Everyone is suppose to be ready for their Kingdom by preparing Christ's Assembly; making sure the Body is in great shape. This is very scriptural! What is the hold up! All while kings and priests are being slain for Christ's name sake, the rest of My assembly is worried about a rapture." thus saith *The Lord.*

Revelation 1:6

6 And hath made us kings and priests unto God and his Father; to him be glory and dominion for ever and ever. Amen

Luke 21:12-13

12But before all this, they will seize you and persecute you. On account of My name, they will deliver you to the synagogues and prisons, and they will bring you before kings and governors. 13This will be your opportunity to serve as a witness.

God does things his way or no way at all! People's brains are their shortcomings, because God will not compromise his truths about our salvation over brain matter. Do you understand that millions of people are brain washed, and that's far more then God is willing, but who's counting? Considering He said He is not willing for even one to perish for lack of knowledge; let alone by their own speculations.

2 Peter 3:9

9The Lord is not slow to fulfill His promise as some understand slowness, but is patient with you, not wanting anyone to perish, but everyone to come to repentance.

Hosea 4:6

6 My people are destroyed for lack of knowledge: because thou hast rejected knowledge, I will also reject thee, that thou shalt be no priest to me: seeing thou hast forgotten the law of thy God, I will also forget thy children.

God does not operate under speculations. The brain is a spectator of the soul. The spirit tells the soul what to do; what's good and natural. The soul understands, not naturally, but by God's gift of understanding that proves everything. Perfectly! The brain is the last to operate in God's Holy Manifold. Have you ever been brain washed before? Well this isn't brain washing or holy brain soap, so relax and just enjoy the ride.

Faith is the operation, and true faith is uncompromising. You might as well surrender and be free by trusting in God, then be tormented by condemnation of a relentless soul that is unfaithful and unchastised, because it chooses to make it's own choices and decisions, and refuses profusely not to surrender or to be second persons. Well that's the way! Ok so demonstration; God is the way, the truth, and the life. No abominations and no liars, only chemistry. You don't think it's fair? Well silence from a real prophet isn't fair either. Mercy isn't about you, it's about what he paid for and internal/eternal gratitude. Last but not least, some of us are chosen; not everyone is chosen! How many times do you have to be told your special? Don't tell me you're afraid of a little power, isn't that what you've been looking for? You have access to unlimited power, come on sinners! Confession releases you from condemnation on every spiritual part of God and yourself.

Proverbs 28:13

Whoever conceals his transgressions will not prosper, but he who confesses and forsakes them will obtain mercy.

One day I was cleaning and I heard a voice say *"confession is 9/10ths of God's law and possession is 9/10ths of Satan's."*

So if your still miserable then you're not surrendered or being a responsible believer to the Triune God. When we are living in sin without any attempts to repent we should feel a strong conviction by the Holy Spirit, if your not convicted in any form then you do not have the Helper. The Holy Spirit works to pursue you diligently, who goes over and over sin until you abandon sin and what opposes the Holy Spirit.

Galatians 5:22-25 — But the fruit of the Spirit is love, joy, peace, longsuffering, kindness, goodness, faithfulness, gentleness, self-control. Against such there is no law. And those who are Christ's have crucified the flesh with its passions and desires. If we live in the Spirit, let us also walk in the Spirit.

John 16:7-8 — Nevertheless I tell you the truth. It is to your advantage that I go away; for if I do not go away, the Helper will not come to you; but if I depart, I will send Him to you. And when He has come, He will convict the world of sin, and of righteousness, and of judgment.

Christ resumes (to pursue something after a pause or interruption) the responsibility for his faithful and true servants. You see your addiction is not the problem your having, it's the personal abomination against God. How many times did you surrender? And how many visions, and fellowship Holy Spirit conversations have you had recently? Exactly, God doesn't change... **you do!**

Proverbs 28:9

He who turns away his ear from listening to the law, Even his prayer is an abomination

Luke 6:46

"Why do you call Me, 'Lord, Lord,' and do not do what I say?

Titus 1:16

They profess to know God, but by their deeds they deny Him, being detestable and disobedient and worthless for any good deed.

Spiritual abominations are derived from a sinner who surrenders initially and then retreats with no spiritual armor or under wire (the voice of the Holy Spirit) because he fantasizes about the dream of being set free, without doing any of the work. You have to seek God with your whole heart or he will never gain your whole heart, and that's pretty heartless to offer up part of your heart for spiritual gain. There's no partial gain with God! So then why should there be with you? Get real, literally, physically, and spiritually! There is no redo's in God's salvation, you're either in or you're out, you either have salvation or you don't! Make sense? When you surrender you're suppose to diligently seek God for the Holy Spirit who is your Confidant, your Redeemer, and your Best Friend. Your suppose to worship like your life depends on it, because in God's eyes it does! And last but certainly not least, you absolutely must, it **IS** a must that you commune with a Holy God. He requires it of us as "fellow" believers and "fellow" worshippers. What would be so fellow about it; about us, if there was no fellowship?

Proverbs 1:27-28

…27When your dread comes like a storm And your calamity comes like a whirlwind, When distress and anguish come upon you. 28"Then they will call on me, but I will not answer; They will seek me diligently but they will not find me,29Because they hated knowledge And did not choose the fear of the LORD

Proverbs 8:17

"I love those who love me; And those who diligently seek me will find me.

1 Samuel 8:18

"Then you will cry out in that day because of your king whom you have chosen for yourselves, but the LORD will not answer you in that day."

This verse in Samuel has a three dimensional meaning to my own experiences with God, before I started hearing his voice and was truly saved. I adhered to unprofitable teachings about God and became convinced or brainwashed on filtered scriptures. This "god" that I "chose" for myself never answered me, never answered my prayers, I wasn't even drawn to him by any spiritual feelings of hunger or thirst, and most importantly there was no love coming or going! I couldn't even tell myself God loved me, because his love was of no relevance at the time, as I was spiritually denied, so there was no spiritual awakening to confirm the very evident attributes of the living, loving, very merciful, triune God.

This verse speaks volumes to my heart, because as I mentioned before, so many people go to church every Sunday, and they believe they are following all the rules, but what they are **NOT** doing is singling their selves out, their saying to themselves they have the helper but where is your help, they say they are hungry yet they are fed by foolery and greed, they say they have discernment but they don't know the day nor hour in which they live, they say they seek after a loving, kind, merciful God, but they will not find him where they are because a multitude of " saved" Christians don't know saved unless it's on their terms. They worship "their" god who saves **BY** deliverance rather then worshipping the True God who saves **THROUGH** repentance, chastisement, strong rebuke, and fire! The fear of the Almighty Lord their God, is past and not present! They seek to destroy the wisdom of the Ancient One who was and is and is to come, and turn over knowledge to desolate and unto some even perverse men of lies and iniquity with no shame, unto their unknowing of their own shame, that has now become the transgressions of the congregation. Why you might ask? Because a " **DELIVERED"** soul" doesn't say sanctified, or redeemed. Their "salvation" derives from an equivalent notion that saved, sanctified, redeemed, and even **DELIVERED** comes from the same aspect of gratuity as saving grace, by He who saves endlessly. Yet the honor to be gained by peer mortals is inequivalent and unfathomable to real searchers and truth seekers, when their mission is finding Him in spirit and in truth, not just in church on Sunday after you shook the preacher's hand, who is leading you to believe that God is passionate about grace and he lives to serve us in all our ways, that he covered our debt, and how time changes nothing, and now we are all free to live our cowardly and unrepentant "saved" lives, as long as we believe we are free. Wow sounds like a horror story straight out of the Catacombs! Deliverance was never man made and redemption was never open to the conscious for their belief system, that's not how this works. Where's the humility brought to you by the **POWER** of His saving grace? There are keys in which a believer must know wherefore and whence he was saved. Determination never saved anybody unless you are Christ, and man doesn't stand a chance in saving one another, not in this day and age.

Compare your battles with those of the Arcadian, or those who roamed the earth as Father Abram, to relinquish his love and loyalty to his master, his God, his friend. Unravel the journeys of so many others who lost their days and nights in fight and quarrel to stand with one another under the mighty blue sky, to roam and not be alone. Understand the iniquity and shame brought forth all at once, on the mighty name of the Prince of Peace, our Lord and Savior Jesus Christ. These names have not all been documented, but that doesn't mean they don't exist, you see God has it all written down and nothing, I repeat nothing goes unnoticed, and that's by the grace of God too...bet you didn't know that. The forewarning here is to be more like Christ, we have to search the mind of Christ, and you're not going to get there picking each other's brains for clues and answers, that's small talk! Keep the jibber-jabber to a minimum. God still speaks in small still places; your own heart, but you must forward all that other stuff to another place, where it cannot be found until your recollection of who God all Mighty truly is, and it comes by hearing who **HE...** says **HE** is! Not the other way around. The Word still breathes like fire, and the fire He produces provides an unquenchable desire, with passion to grow closer and grow in knowledge and wisdom of who He says He is. If you don't have the fire that surpasses all worldly envisions of the God Almighty, then you will never truly know him or the peace that surpasses all understandings. To know Him is to love Him. Come be apart of it brother, God is worth waiting for!

Proverbs 20:24

A man's steps are determined by the LORD, so how can anyone understand his own way?

Romans 11:33

33 O, the depth of the riches of the wisdom and knowledge of God! How unsearchable His judgments, and untraceable His ways! 34"Who has known the mind of the Lord? Or who has been His counselor?" 35"Who has given so much to God, that God should repay him?

Notice that His ways are **UNTRACEABLE!** So how then can the mass multitudes have God and salvation so mapped out? I'll tell you why, because it's under their own conditioning and their own reproof . A saddler is fond of his conditioning and handiwork, but the performance of the stallion depends on the rider. Needless to say, the brain works in mysterious ways, so then how much more the greatness and equality of the Living God, who subdues these mantras of man made religion? God is not an offering, offered to people on their terms of endearment, He is justifiably concerned with their religious practices, and quite frankly smitten with foolery from indoctrinated images of The Great Elohim!

Job 15:8 Have you heard the secret of God? and do you restrain wisdom to yourself?

Job 36:22 Behold, God exalts by his power: who teaches like him?

We are not to serve God by obtaining his mercy and grace through our **OWN** beliefs and congruence (compatibility) to God, that is truancy to God!

Proverbs 28:26

He who trusts in his own heart is a fool, But he who walks wisely will be delivered.

Proverbs 3:5

Trust in the LORD with all thine heart; and lean not unto thine own understanding.

We are suppose to have crossed over that threshold by now and be indulging and endeavoring in the mercies, in the multitudes of his graciousness, and in the prosperity of his spiritual relinquishments and attributions. Not having our hand out, waving at him from the door. so to speak. Where are our morals? Where is the respect for the Living God who once came as an offering for peace and greatness among his people and captives? It's so overbearing when a world relinquishes their love on their own attributions and on their own sincerity for the cares of the world. Yet we are under the same Son that has given over his life as a ransom for all mankind, to depart from this nature, to depart from this worldly wisdom, and honor filled society. More over we became a part of Christ when He died on the cross, and **ALL** humanity has a **PART** in God's truth whether we like it or not. We may not have a say - so in the morals and respects of other people, but we do have a right in Christ to take a stand on what we will not stand for, and that's debauchery, carousing, and failing to operating in God's unfailing love and not your own. As far as I can see the love this world owns is sickening, it's blasphemous, it's a carouser and a murder; yet it's contagious like a morbid lurking death sentence slid under the cover of love! It is stifling at the murder rates among so called "loved ones" which gives a new meaning to " I love you to death", **NO!** Christ loves us unto death, and He proved it with His own life, and not by taking another's! This so called love has adorn this world as an earthen vesture that leaves no room to grow, as it holds back the unknown so that it doesn't get erased in all it's falsehood. This "love" does not know it's place and has no place in the circle of life, because it's a taker of life and not a giver of life, it's tormentorous and undeniably cruel. This is a no man's land, because no true man who is knowledgeable and takes heart, would sustain this inoperable and inopportune decision to operate under man's law, under man's righteousness, man's strongholds, and man's courageousness! It's a power struggle to be first and not last, that should tell you who and where these humans operate from, because in God's Kingdom the first is the last and the last is the first. Take note and take heed, because this might be your last chance and whether is comes to you as a surprise or not, God's commandments are over every man woman and child, so that you will know how to act accordingly, when transpiring pernicious wolves come to the feed, to steal, and take away right out from under you.

Mark 4:15 And these are the ones along the path, where the word is sown; when they hear, Satan immediately comes and takes away the word which is sown in them. And these in like manner are the ones sown upon rocky ground, who, when they hear the word, immediately receive it with joy; and they have no root in themselves, but endure for a while; then, when tribulation or persecution arises on account of the word, immediately they fall away. And others are the ones sown among thorns; they are those who hear the word, but the cares of the world, and the delight in riches, and the desire for other things, enter in and choke the word, and it proves unfruitful. But those that were sown upon the good soil are the ones who hear the word and accept it and bear fruit, thirtyfold and sixtyfold and a hundredfold.

Jesus also said in the book of *John 15 regarding salvation; "If a man does not abide in me, he is cast forth as a branch and withers; and the branches are gathered, thrown into the fire, and burned."* Ultimately what is at stake if Satan takes away the Word of God is our salvation. Without the Word of God abiding and taking root in our heart we cannot bear fruit, be disciples, or inherit eternal life. So if you're surprised don't be, as these revelations have been documented before time and is proved true by the same congregations claiming truth and salvation, yet are cowering, rolling in the fields playfully, carousing with carousers and are amongst all those who are here to deliver you up to the synagogues of Satan! Well I'd say these ticklers have picked an operable time to play guessing games and to tend to their herds after they have already gone astray. You take for keeps and live close to the edge, you build mountains when you were meant to move them! Make no mistake about it, God is still very much in charge and does reign forevermore! Nothing is lost that wasn't meant to be lost and no one has gone to far astray that God cannot bring him back, unless he doesn't want to be brought back, but how would he know how far is to far, or what it is he would be coming back to? If the truth is so manipulated, turned backwards, and inside out that he is being blind sided in every aspect and area of his life because his "teachers" are under rule and demand not to speak about homosexuality but gay rights, and not to bring about division with the sword (Word), but that everyone will be accepted as they are, in believing there's no room for reform or retribution, that tormented souls are a thing of the past and what lye's beneath now is just anger issues, depression, anxiety, and schizophrenia; in which they have the cure-all...medicine.

1 Timothy 5:20

...19Do not entertain an accusation against an elder, except on the testimony of two or three witnesses. 20But those who persist in sin should be rebuked in front of everyone, so that the others will stand in fear of sin. 21I solemnly charge you before God and Christ Jesus and the elect angels to maintain these principles without bias, and to do nothing out of partiality.

Congratulations! They have once again mapped out God's contributions to the world and they are free to go tell the world what they think about it since they hold all the knowledge and understanding, or so they think. Boy that brain does get people into a lot of trouble! Evidently it's true what the Lord has said to me; *"seeing is not always believing because perception is not always reality." thus saith the Lord.*

Romans 12:1

1Therefore I urge you, brothers, on account of God's mercy, to offer your bodies as living sacrifices, holy and pleasing to God, which is your spiritual service of worship. 2Do not be conformed to this world, but be transformed by the renewing of your mind. Then you will be able to discern what is the good, pleasing, and perfect will of God. 3For by the grace given me I say to every one of you: Do not think of yourself more highly than you ought, but think of yourself with sober judgment, according to the measure of faith God has given you.

Romans 1:26

26For this reason God gave them over to dishonorable passions. Even their women exchanged natural relations for unnatural ones.27Likewise, the men abandoned natural relations with women and burned with lust for one another. Men committed indecent acts with other men, and received in themselves the due penalty for their error. 28Furthermore, since they did not see fit to acknowledge God, He gave them up to a depraved mind, to do what should not be done.

Leviticus 18:22

'You shall not lie with a male as one lies with a female; it is an abomination.

Revelations 21:8

But the fearful, and unbelieving, and the abominable, and murderers, and whoremongers, and sorcerers, and idolaters, and all liars, shall have their part in the lake which burneth with fire and brimstone: which is the second death.

James 1:11-12

…11For the sun rises with scorching heat and withers the plant; its flower falls and its beauty is lost. So too, the rich man will fade away in the midst of his pursuits. 12Blessed is the man who perseveres under trial, because when he has stood the test, he will receive the crown of life that God has promised to those who love Him.

Exodus 20:6

but showing loving kindness to thousands, to those who love Me and keep My commandment.

Didn't I tell you we will **ALL** have a **PART** in God's truth?

Section Fifteen

God Speaks!

God has a word for some of you. To say that God does not speak to you unless it's written down and found in scripture, is like unto the same as saying someone doesn't know God! As God lives and breaths eternally, He speaks just as much!

Volumes could **NEVER** contain, so wise up. All the gifts of The Spirit are expression-able. God's expressional ability is in places that no scripture can explain, or obtain.

Through my prophetic gift and anointing God spoke this to me;

*"I live where I live, and I go where I go. I say what I say. I do not have to proof read before I say what I say, like a miscreant. The Holy scriptures is where I have been. Do not get that confused, there is nothing wrong with showing up where I belong. Where I once was I still belong. To say God is His scriptures is to say that **I AM** is awfully little. There is no way that I finished talking at the end of the Bible! I wrote the book, I read the book, live where I live and go where I go, that is an*

expression for you! It is not live where I live and go where I've been. Have faith sinner your life is in good hands. Now why would I say that If proof reading was a real example of God expected faith? Then your faith would hold no future! Do I uphold you to where you have been or who you once were? Of course not that would be a horrible example of a just God! Live where I live and go where I go . At the end of the day we are only where we are regardless of where we've been.

If Faith can move mountains, but it cannot leave a time zone, then how much would we really be compromising? Then what are Heaven's Messengers here for, if no one can hear them? Well there has got to be some purpose for them!

Then what are you humans here for? For if I "invented humans truly" then where is their expiration date? (everything invented has a expiration date, That is what your assuming right?) Or are you saying I just do not know what to say them anymore? Can they out "spoke" me? (spoke as a past term, considering what people say about God only speaking through one way) What way would that be? Enlighten Me! Did Elijah read the scriptures and become strong? Did Moses read the scriptures into the Holy Of Holies? Afraid not. We would still be concubines and only literature. Your pastors need to wake up, because where God lives there's nobody there! They are all stuck in Biblical sororities of one faith, just all in different time zones! Scriptures are for reading and recording. It is Heaven's recompense to the Elite Chosen Ones of the Bible so they would not be forgotten or have labored in vain. As much I love The Word, it is truly a scriptural relief, that proves Isaiah, Ezekiel, John, and Jacob (Israel) are prophets of Jehovah by dispensation Of His Holy Spirit and not the proof reading, as if those pages are to speak as a Heavenly Host. I heard them, I wrote them. Nowhere does it say I have been right here waiting for you, where I will only be and can only hear you, and if you need Me, you know where to find Me! Where in the Word does it say anything about the scripture (the actual word on the pages) talking? Which way would that be in? And in which language? I do not speak Indian, Arminian, Greek, Spanish, et cetera, et cetera. When you are uncreated you do not have a native tongue. I speak Faith!

God is not the Author of confusion, is He? So then where is His native tongue? It is opening and closing the mouths of many!" Thus says The Great Elohim.*

So if I'm guilty of sneaking up on God in a different time zone,where He apparently lives, then that is the chance I'm willing to take and price I'm willing to pay!

Repentance

Jeremiah 5:3

O LORD, do not Your eyes look for truth? You have smitten them, But they did not weaken; You have consumed them, But they refused to take correction. They have made their faces harder than rock; They have refused to repent

Acts 3:19 " Repent, then, and turn to God, so that your sins may be wiped out, that times of refreshing may come from the Lord."

So you've been baptized but have not repented of your sins? How's that working out for you? Without repentance your only coming out of that baptism a wet sinner. That's why the Word says Repent and then be baptized. That water is not magical and you can't depend on the water to change you. The baptism of The Holy Spirit, now that's when we are baptized with fire, and that is the power to change. I asked God how can I know I'm saved and that I'm baptized by the

Holy Spirit? He replied; "**REPENTANCE!**" Wow less truly is more! God doesn't change.

Jesus Christ is the same yesterday, and today and forever. Hebrews 13:8

While the Lord walked this earth He preached "repent or perish!"

So many people say they are waiting on God to deliver them.

Why would God delay your repentance? He commands us with urgency saying in *2 Corinthians 6:2 "Behold **NOW** is the accepted time behold **NOW** is the day of salvation."*

*The Apostles said "Do not delay, I tell you **NOW** is the time of God's favor **NOW** is the day of salvation."* If the warning was this serious and urgent back in the biblical days, then how much more now that the future is here? For on this very night your life may be required of you! Do not harden your heart or allow your soul to be vexed cold!

Proverbs 28:13-14

13 Whoever conceals his transgressions will not prosper, but he who confesses and forsakes them will obtain mercy. 14 Blessed is the one who fears the Lord always, but whoever hardens his heart will fall into calamity 2 Corinthians

5:17-18

17 Therefore if any man be in Christ, he is a new creature: old things are passed away; behold, all things are become new.

How many have not put their childish things away?

How many of us are still returning to our vomit as a dog?

Proverbs 26:11 "as a dog returns to it's vomit, so fools repeat their folly."

1 Corinthians 13:11 "but when I became a man I put away my childish things and put away my childish ways."

As faithful as a cigarette calls to a smoker, how much more will God call to you? What will be your excuse in that fearful day when He will require an answer of you over all your rejecting Him? God's deliverance and healing is perfect in all his ways, so what will be your excuse for all your delay?

You have to commit to one of two choices, who you are, or who God is. Are you going to be the wick or the light? Our arms are to short to box with God, so why all the contending? God moves quickly and swiftly, so if we start to sleep on who he is we will have trouble in paradise. When we don't surrender fully to God, we are just laughing in the face of danger, which is like a slap in Gods face! We are damoiseaus/damsels in distress who should be faithfully waiting without doubt that He's only tarrying over our survival; but when it's time He will come! These are the end days and we all should now prepare to be quickened by the

Spirit, illuminated, and moving faster. We are to make sure we are always working and improving with great rapport. God did not bring us this far to slit our throats with the same sword he provided us with, or hang us by all the rope he extended to us through his grace!

Pain is not a stopping point, it's an opportunity to dig deeper. Christ holds us, love sustains us, and faith serves us.

The golden whistler is someone who stands in the middle of two people and says "let's fight!" As the golden whistler, you're not only the one refereeing this fight, but your the one who called it, from beginning to end. That's a double standard in God's eyes. God doesn't cage fight, he already holds the title, with vengeance close behind! We can contend with each other that it's over, that God already saved everyone, and you can choose to stay as faithful as you want to the heretic saying that "once saved always saved" is practical faith, but *Exodus 15:3 says " The* **LORD** *is a man of war, the* **LORD** *is his name."*

God will wage war against the lawless ones, the ones who are rebellious and practicing iniquity. As God lives, judgement has always been over the mass multitude of a rebelling people or nation. No matter how beautiful, talented, young, or old, there will always be blood shed in the wages of sin, in hopes of waking people up in the mass multitudes! People don't now what their loosing if their snoozing.

How can you know if your losing a battle if your sleeping, let alone what war or "round" you are in? Much of the great apostasy has already happened, but the majority is still waiting for it to begin! Doesn't that show you how faithful God is? To defend a war that is unfairly going it's own way, with nothing to hope in and no armor for self defense?

The Lord said to me *"If one of my sheep goes astray, I will not continue tending to my flock, I will leave the 99 and pursue the one! You can't always runaway from the one coming after you."*

As I was going my own way, The Lord pulled me out of a whirlwind and began speaking to me from deep down in his heart saying;

"Katie I would rather leave the 99, and pursue the one who fell asleep under the Sheppard's own watch. Do you not know that the owner would require an answer of the Sheppard, for even one who went astray?" says the Lord.

Thank God, we have a faithful Sheppard! God of Heavenly armies says no man left behind. As the Bible declares he is not willing for even one to parish. To say He is not willing is not to say that it will not happen. People do perish, that's why repent or parish was an important part of Jesus's ministry. The truth is; not everyone is going to heaven. The code of war is kill or be killed, is it not? In War God will **NOT** be mocked! In war He will either defend you or condemn you, it won't matter if your knee deep in your Bible or hand grenades at that point, because He has already chosen His platoon faithfully!

Refusing to repent can be a very permanent and close call for your life, especially if you are spiritual, that's even more dangerous. Even though Satan is very cunning, he cannot interfere with your free will, so blaming him will never be a good enough excuse to God, as God always gives you a way out. The choice initially is always yours. Some of those initial choices include, reading the Bible, repenting, and living faithful to God. No one walks away from God because repentance was impossible for them, they walk away because the desires of their flesh are more important to them, which is selfish. For if we claim the blood of God's precious son just so we can parade around under protection from the enemy, and without repenting and being washed clean by the blood, we are charged by the Kingdom of God! This is very unconstitutional in Heaven. Do you realize how prideful this is to God? Many will beg for mercy for this exact sin.

Many people who claim the blood of Christ are going to be in a lot of trouble according to Hebrews *10:26-27*

26 For if we sin willfully after that we have received the knowledge of the truth, there remaineth no more sacrifice for sins,

27 But a certain fearful looking for of judgment and fiery indignation, which shall devour the adversaries.

WOW THAT SCREAMS TERRIFING! If you know what Christ has done for you as much as living a sinless life for you, suffering God's wrath for you, being crucified unto death, spending three days in the earth, and being resurrected unto life, all for you; and you don't work repentance in your life, it is now **YOU** who crucifies the **LORD!**

Every thing I just mentioned is the exact interpretation of John 3:16.

To believe Christ 1. Is the Son of God, 2. Died for sin, and 3. Resurrected unto life.

People say they do believe John 3:16 so now they're saved, without knowledge that Hebrews 10:26 goes hand in hand. For if you do not repent of premeditated sin then John 3:16 no longer applies to you, and it is now **YOU** who crucifies the Son of God by the same iniquities and principalities that nailed him to the cross.

What choice are you leaving him? To parade around under Heavenly hosts and not just a God, but a Holy, Holy, Holy, Father of Christ? Should God have to relive even a second of his pain? Seeing people confess His sacrifices and cover themselves in His precious blood, then live a life in ruin? **REPENT** then!

Wash your robes! Thou shall **NOT** tempt the **LORD** thy **GOD!**

NO BIBLE, NO WORSHIP, NO PRAISE, NO CONFESSIONS, NO PLEADING THE BLOOD OF CHRIST, will deliver you, if you live without surrender, or working repentance! Only the grace of God, who ordained neatly the form in which we are to be conformed to.

Life is hard enough and the time has been shortened. Do not force the Lord to use restraint, that's learning the hard way in layman terms, and trust me from experience; it's not easy!

No matter how strong we are, we will never move mountains in our own strength, but we can allow that same mountain to make us strong.

Sinners sin, backsliders backslide, but as long as there is time left there is rope left.

As God lives, God gives.

Mosiah 4:10-12

10 And again, believe that ye must repent of your sins and forsake them, and humble yourselves before God; and ask in sincerity of heart that he would forgive you; and now, if you believe all these things see that ye do them.

11 And again I say unto you as I have said before, that as ye have come to the knowledge of the glory of God, or if ye have known of his goodness and have tasted of his love, and have received a remission of your sins, which causeth such exceedingly great joy in your souls, even so I would that ye should remember, and always retain in remembrance, the greatness of God, and your own nothingness, and his goodness and long-suffering towards you, unworthy creatures, and humble yourselves even in the depths of humility, calling on the name of the Lord daily, and standing steadfastly in the faith of that which is to come, which was spoken by the mouth of the angel.

12 And behold, I say unto you that if ye do this ye shall always rejoice, and be filled with the love of God, and always retain a remission of your sins; and ye shall grow in the knowledge of the glory of him that created you, or in the knowledge of that which is just and true.

Trinity

God is three distinct individuals. God the Father, God the Son, and The Holy Spirit of God. All three together make up one God. The word "trinity" comes from the word "tri" meaning three and unity: meaning one.

1 Corinthians 13:14, 1 Corinthians 8:6, 2Corinthians3:17, Colossians 2:9,

Isaiah 9:6, Isaiah 44:6 John 1:14, John 10:30, Luke 1:35, Matt 1: 23, Matt 28:19,

Matt 3:16-17, John 14:16-17, 1 John 5:7-8, Col 1:15-17.

Millions of souls have no knowledge of the mystery of the Trinity that is hidden in God. God is indeed one, but there are three deities or Supreme Rulers who make up the one true God. We should acknowledge them for who they are, where each one lives and what role each has as God.

If you want a relationship with a very personal God, then your going to have to know Him! Don't be afraid of getting to know each being of God. He loves when we are curious and meditate on who He is! When I was a babe in Christ and new to hearing his' voices (as he speaks in many forms) I quickly realized there were many ways he would communicate with me.

Don't be afraid to ask God questions if you don't understand. I was on a mission to understand the mysterious Trinity, and the truth about who my Heavenly Father is. If you step out in faith to go deeper with God trying to understand the Holy Trinity, let me be the first to tell you, our minds cannot fathom the whole mystery. You can try and I encourage you, but don't get to carried away and lose focus of the God who is **NOT** the author of confusion. *1 Corinthians 14:33.*

Simplicity is best sometimes.

The Father

The Father is the God Head . The Most High. Some people pray to the Savior but we are told to pray to the Father (by Christ Himself) yet in the name of Christ our Savior. Most people say "the Savior is the Father" according to Isaiah 9:6, but it's a little more complex then that my dear. I'm sure there is no harm in calling Him your Father, after all the scripture says Everlasting Father.

In ancient history servants would call masters "my Lord" does that mean this "master" was thee Lord? Of course not.

So yes Christ is an everlasting Father, but the Bible says he sits at the right hand of The Father, also he prayed to his Heavenly Father, specifying Christ is not the Heavenly Father. The only problem is people neglect the Father and The Holy Spirit unconsciously.

Not only is it tragic, but your missing out on God in his entirety! Don't be lazy, seek God's face and you will see He has three. Each one will melt your heart.

The Father has always been mysterious to us, as we picture Him with White wooly Hair and beard, looking like a grandfather. Most people reported seeing Christ's face, but the Bible says no one has seen the Father at any time, and certainly have not lived to talk about it!

Jehovah is the name of the first everlasting omnipotent God, meaning **I AM** That **I AM**.

Does Moses and the burning bush ring a bell? That should tell you who **I AM** is. Searching for the Father may be a challenge for almost all Christians. Not because it's harder to know Him, but because Jehovah (Father) doesn't receive His glory from men, who are literally selfish for not thanking Jehovah (The Father) for everything He is and has done! He is truly jealous for us, and who we worship.

No one should have to balance the Kingdoms worship because holy rollers pride themselves on being spiritual, and worshipping the Savior in designer clothes with designer handbags, singing like they're in a talent show. Shame shame. If they had the knowledge to be honorable by The

Most High, then why don't they worship the Father at His gates? What I'm saying is do you want to make the Father jealous over all your worship of His son? Christ said in the word that He did not come to be served but to serve. He also said do not bow down to me or pray to me but to your Heavenly Father. I understand He is King and we should praise and thank Him daily! Just don't forget the One who made this all possible; Jehovah Father Of Love.

I cannot imagine how Jesus feels after getting praised for all things His Father has done for our recognition, and still does for us to witness to, and give Him the Glory for!

Jehovah beats His staph and the whole world shakes.

"Praise Jesus!"

Jehovah cleans the oceans water, and puts it in it's direct place.

"Praise Your name Yeshua Hamashiach !"

The blind regain their sight and the lame talk.

"Praise the Lord Jesus Christ!"

There is spiritual and there is symmetrical. I don't remember when The Father became symmetrical with His answers. When God formed man you out of sand or a rib, was it holy? Or is it just God who is Holy? For example, His Word formed all things created, so who is the Creator of the Universe? Him Or His Word? I understand that the

Word was God, but what people don't understand is God is
a **title** for **FATHER, SON, HOLY SPIRIT**. Yet Jesus is not
FATHER, SON, HOLY SPIRIT. For every creation there
is a trusted creator with passion and virtue. Jehovah is that
One! The Word was sent forth by God the Father regardless
of how you look at it, God the Father is the Most High,
therefore everything belongs to him.

There is always something that has come here and has left,
or literally risen to Heaven.

That was Yeshua. (son of God / son of man) .

Now I'll help you differentiate worshipping Jehovah over
Yeshua, and the doctrine over the dispensation.

God the Father is jealous over His' worship and praise. It
belongs to Him only for He alone is God! For He **ALONE**
is God! God doesn't share or save His glory for no one! No
One! That means the flesh, even if He was sent by God.
I know its hard to wrap your brain around but it makes
perfect sense. The triune God is very magnificent, but you
cannot take away from the source of it all, the Head and
Creator of His Magnificence, and give it all to Yeshua the
Son of God. That would be to challenge The Great Elohim,
by giving more worship, praise, honor, prayer, and all "His'"
glory to His son. Hence my saying, neither Father nor Son
should have to balance the Kingdom's worship. That's not
fair, and not how it works!

The Bible doesn't say Jesus is Father, Son, and Holy spirit.
The Bible says God is Father, Son, and Holy Spirit. God is

a Title. There is One higher then The Son, but non higher then the Father. That's why He is the Most High God. Jesus said "I'm going to the Father," "The Father prepared a place," "The Father will send one like me in my name," The Father's will be done not mine," "pray to the Father in Heaven," "Get behind me Satan you are an offence to me and my Father."

Father !Father! Father!

The Father doesn't expunge anything Christ has done, or any service His friends choose to do in praise and worship. If you truly love God as you say, and are His family, then how can Christ be your everything? It was El Shaddai who manifested this family, who made Heaven and Earth fear Him and tremble at His Holy countenance. Trust me He did not disappear and become the Savior. God's throne is still in the Heavenly places. Not even the King of the Jews, Anointed One, consecrated to the Most High God, will ever take the Fathers place. Yahweh alone is to be worshipped!

1st of Ten Commandments, Thou shall have no other gods before me.

Philippians 2:10-11

10 that at the name of Jesus every knee should bow, of those in heaven, and of those on earth, and of those under the earth, 11 and that every tongue should confess that Jesus Christ is Lord, to the glory of God the Father.

*Mark 10:39 you will indeed drink the cup that I drink and with the baptism I am baptized with you will be baptized but to sit on my right hand and on my left is **NOT** mine to give but it is for those whom it is prepared*

So you see Christ is the denoting expression of his Father, and we must relinquish our love on The Father in such a way that there is no confusion or challenges in who we are and who we are to be worshipping.

The Holy Spirit is another expression of God's love for us, as is for the Son of the Living God. He is also a maker and creator of new things in regards to hope, future, new names, and new creations by which we are born in harmony and synchronize with the One who is Holy, Holy, Holy. I am personally saved through the dispensation of the Holy Spirit of God, and I am head over hills in love with Him. Operating in true faith and not religion, living charismatically and joyous by the attributions of His Holy Spirit, and confirming them with concord fruits.

The Holy Spirit is quite mysterious, but the explanations of his qualities are superveloce. I am dedicated to my own personal search in finding the Holy Spirit's ransom for my life and salvation, as I know he is not exempt from the service provided to our Heavenly Father and all his riches. I am more then willing to take that leap of faith, to dig deeper amongst the mounds of authoritative authorship, to become closer in listening to the educative discerning power, in relinquishing my contributions to this deity of all consuming power, who holds the narrative sediment in

God's love for me, and proves everything needs a purpose. That's called a relationship, and that's where we find Him!

1 Corinthians 6:9-11

9 Know ye not that the unrighteous shall not inherit the kingdom of God? Be not deceived: neither fornicators, nor idolaters, nor adulterers, nor effeminate, nor abusers of themselves with mankind,

10 Nor thieves, nor covetous, nor drunkards, nor revilers, nor extortioners, shall inherit the kingdom of God.

11 And such were some of you: but ye are washed, but ye are sanctified, but ye are justified in the name of the Lord, and by the Spirit of our God.

The Kingdom of God and The Kingdom of Heaven are surprisingly different. You see the Kingdom of God resides within you, as the beautiful Holy Spirit and gift of Christ's inheritance, if you choose to live faithfully and not among practices of abominations.

The second differentiation of the Kingdoms is such a worldly explanation, that literally the Kingdom is where Christ lives, and where we spend our eternity with Him. Yet God says; God is God Omnipotent, and he lives among the redemption of the redeemed. Heaven is a whole lot of places, more and more everyday. More and more every minute a sinner repents of his selfishness, then the whole Kingdom of God rejoices and imparts the Holy Spirit unto those who turn around and face Him with their own sins! By His good graces our sins are blotted out, only when we repent and seek His gracious face in His graces. That is our God given fate!

Acts 2:38

38Peter replied, **"Repent and be baptized,** *every one of you, in the name of Jesus Christ for the* **forgiveness of your sins, and you will receive the gift of the Holy Spirit.**

The Holy, Holy, Holy Spirit of the Living God does not come to dwell within someone who is still practicing sin. Even if he professes "Jesus Christ is Lord!" from the roof tops. That is **NOT** what God is asking for, that's what God considers blasphemers, because they speak with no knowledge and are among the perpetrators who profess the Living God as their Savior and Redeemer, yet they are among the spiritual abominable! That is **NOT** holy worship, it is unsightly and unfaithful. Do you think God wants confusion amongst His repented holy revival? It's absolutely blasphemous in the house of the Lord!

Don't you realize that even Satan and his elected are completely aware that to worship Christ is not to acknowledge Him, but to obey His commands and statutes that His Heavenly Father gave to Him and He gave to you? Unbelief is just as much of an abomination then a person who believes that He is who He says He is, and continues in iniquity, claiming they are "saved" by the Lord! The Lord doesn't save people by their good works, so how much more will the Lord not save those who not "just" commit iniquity, but **PRACTICE** iniquity?

The Lord sends the Helper initially, very very initially, to stir your faith and make sure your faithful and accountable. The Helper is not the one that turns you, your welcome to come and go freely, as you please.

The Helper comes to stir your confidence in who God says He is and who you believe He says He is.

Ephesians 1:13-14 In him you also, when you heard the word of truth, the gospel of your salvation, and believed in him, were sealed with the promised Holy Spirit, who is the guarantee of our inheritance until we acquire possession of it, to the praise of his glory.

You wouldn't believe how many people still believe that God is **ALL** things! Does that make sense to you? Just because all paths lead to God doesn't mean God leads to all paths. Don't be confused, the author of confusion lives among you working patiently. People still believe the enemy works for God and that is a lie straight from hell. The enemy works among God, not with God. Oh the parody!

Just because your significant other says your both saved, doesn't mean you have to be ignorant if you don't want to. Let me paint you a beautiful picture of the truth.

God has always been a Savior and a Father, but God wants a daughter who wants exactly what he wants. Now God sent his only son to demonstrate that holy grail relationship, isn't God worthy of that holy grail relationship? Why did Jesus have to demonstrate what God is expecting of his relationships if he would just throw his holy recompense on anyone who professes that Jesus is the Lord? That would be wrong and rude to the Savior, who bore judgment so that the Father could have friends and relationships in his good graces, and not recycle the pattern of what humanity wants over a loving relationship with the Heavenly Father. Don't you want to know how sweet and caring He is? How loving and kind hearted He is? Well don't you!? Then why do you shy away over salvation? "Oh I'm saved!" and that's the end of the conversation, but it tempts God to anger. How did He save you? Don't you know we should magnify the Good Lord by our own servitude of our salvation, Don't you think God wants everyone to know how amazing he is and how totally awesome your relationship with the Savior has been? Or has it? Well if you don't know how close you've become to the Savior Yeshua, or his Father Yahweh, then your relationship could be in serious trouble! God is the Creator and Giver of salvation, not the giver of his sacred blessings of fortitude in self sacrifice, resentment, lying, strife, abominations, or encouraging the abominable, and struggling with medications as sorcerers claim they don't do; but they do. This hurts God deeply, and the pain that God experiences grieves the remarkable Holy Spirit of the Triune God!

Remember Simon the sorcerer didn't get the Holy Spirit by flocking to the Holy Spirit's witnessing power, even being a believer. Simon didn't receive because he was captivated by the power he would be capable of once the Spirit of God descended upon him, and put a price on the Holy Spirit's power, rather then a sacrifice of repentance and surrender. You see that the Apostles had no mercy on him. **NO**, they rebuked him and told him he better pray for what he had been guilty of, lest he parish with his money!

Now as I was painting you a beautiful picture, I turned around to see that you were painting someone else a picture, about a King named Jesus who saves everyone and anyone with or without their relationship with him. Just as the apostles told Simon, I will tell you **REPENT OR PARISH!** Or you will regret listening to what everyone else says.

Judgement And Justice

"People if we expose the lies, have faith in the truth, we will see justice, by God!"

As I had been having vivid dreams rhetorically, I made a stand in my dream saying this statement, encouraging people over this abomination of desolation that is leaving so many humans desolate and killing innumerable. Drugs.

As soon as I said this I woke up, and the presence of not only God but many was felt prominently! I heard a voice say " this is scriptural."

The epidemic of drug abuse, over dosage, and fatal addictions, are all forms of sorcery, by leverage associated with spiritual, and physical levitation. To be "high" if you want me to sugar coat it. But in all actuality this process of spiritual reform is the epitome of what it looks like to worship Satan and the image of the beast.

The desolate imminent trance of sorceries' marketing and targeting, is poverty and inevitably addiction. Sorceries' simulation is "to help" but the spiritual downfall is recluse (hidden) in a endless downward spiral against humanity.

When will man wise up and take a stand against the FDA approved federal dope? What is man afraid to loose? Are these victims collecting compensation for opioid drug abuse? Well they should be. Beat the system don't let the system beat you.

This is a sickness don't forget, but it does not constitute for the ridicule of self sacrifice or rhetoric ploy of human sacrificing! This delusion is an element made hastily by federal rulers and regulators in the physical (human) realm, made spiritually manifest for the rulers of darkness by the rulers of darkness and principalities heir to the prince of the air. Satan in layman's terms.

These principalities are the same ones oppressing and possessing your preachers, judges, doctors, etc. Whether they are able to use insight or are subconsciously unaware of this "spiritual pardon" by the career in which they operate under; God doesn't see it that way. To perform a modern day exorcism by medications, and meditations, is not spiritual reform as this "exorcism" of pain from spiritual, mental, and physical torment is under the scrutiny of the same professionals I mentioned by law. They themselves are suffering from the oppression, depression, and even possession, of demonic spiritual impressions to carry out a satanic agenda. Wherein a house divided cannot stand, because Satan cannot cast out Satan.

Matthew 12:25-28

25 But Jesus knew their thoughts, and said to them: "Every kingdom divided against itself is brought to desolation, and every city or house divided against itself will not stand. 26 If Satan casts out Satan, he is divided against himself. How then will his kingdom stand? 27 And if I cast out demons by Beelzebub, by whom do your sons cast them out? Therefore they shall be your judges. 28 But if I cast out demons by the Spirit of God, surely the kingdom of God has come upon you.

Pain regulation is a disguise and spoof of spiritual incontinence. You should never let your guard down, but continue sifting the dark waters. That is what your spiritual helpers are here for! The spiritual divine attributions are love is patient, love is kind. Is that what the CDC regulators are doing behind close doors to the blindsided victims. Most certainly not! And why is that? I don't know all the side details but one thing is most certain, and that's personal gain. Lets start with abatement, or personal exchange just to name a few abdominal traits. Regardless the illegitimate trade, it's all for gain with financial stigmata. That is the stinger of the locust!

Revelations 9:10

10 And they had tails like unto scorpions, and there were stings in their tails: and their power was to hurt men five months.

For these abominations are death among the dead. For the Tried and True Living God was bruised and smitten by these abominable perversions, and to neglect the Son as your Savior with no remorse in regards to your submission to opioid prescription drugs and worldly medication, is a terrible and risky behavior! Even among the abdominal this is ludicrous, because Jesus didn't scarifies his own life just to be rejected for personal torture. A graven mistake.

1 Corinthians 6:9

Know ye not that the unrighteous shall not inherit the kingdom of God? Be not deceived: neither fornicators, nor idolaters, nor adulterers, nor effeminate, nor abusers of themselves with mankind

No one knows the cost of an abomination. No one living, and no one in the dirt, because of Jesus our Savior! The only one who took the abominations of mankind and settled it so we could all live! So why can't we? Why can't we be free? Why then is there suffering without justice? I'll tell you why, it's because of human refusal, and there is a double standard.

Human's ultimate debate with God is "their is no mercy! & No deliverance!"

There is no mercy because there is no human standard! Is God suppose to exonerate the drunkard, the rapist, or "junkie"? Afraid not, as serious as the Bible is, in all it's seriousness, scripture states precisely in

Revelation 22:15-

15 For without are dogs, and sorcerers, and whoremongers, and murderers, and idolaters, and whosoever loveth and maketh a lie.

Corinthians 6:9-10

9 Know ye not that the unrighteous shall not inherit the kingdom of God? Be not deceived: neither fornicators, nor idolaters, nor adulterers, nor effeminate, nor abusers of themselves with mankind,

10 Nor thieves, nor covetous, nor drunkards, nor revilers, nor extortioners, shall inherit the kingdom of God.

Galatians 5:19-21 19 Now the works of the flesh are evident: sexual immorality,impurity, sensuality, 20 idolatry, sorcery, enmity, strife, jealousy,

fitsof anger, rivalries, dissensions, divisions, 21 envy, drunkenness,orgies, and things like these. I warn you, as I warned you before, that those who do such things will not inherit the kingdom of God.

Ephesians 5:5

5 For this ye know, that no whoremonger, nor unclean person, nor covetous man, who is an idolater, hath any inheritance in the kingdom of Christ and of God

1 Timothy 1:9

9 understanding this, that the law is not laid down for the just but for the lawless and disobedient, for the ungodly and sinners, for the unholy and profane, for those who strike their fathers and mothers, for murderers.

Hebrews 12:14

14 Strive for peace with everyone, and for the holiness without which no one will see the Lord.

Many times through out scripture we are warned! Now does it sound like The gracious God is playing around? **NOT** in the slightest! Some of you have played around far to long, because you think God is so gracious, and he is! But you cannot string Him along by this! The scripture also says God **CANNOT** be mocked. God cannot be broken, so this mending God together in hopes of a supporting God who takes it all away, is all make believe and derision. God stays the same. *Hebrews 13:8 Jesus Christ is the same yesterday and today and forever.*

In layman's terms God does not change to fit your lifestyle, that would be pointless! It would be hard for him to Reign and Rule from the state of **"YOU"** as most are unruly, insubordinate, and perpetual liars; need I say more?

"But drugs addicts are sick, it's a disease." they claim with all certainty, without any regards to the spiritual aspect of this nature, but in reference to their illegitimate and unsightly claims. How is that any different from a drunkard's sickness? If you say disease, is that suppose to change the unchanging Holy Scriptures, that have been settled in Earth as it is in Heaven? Well why didn't you say so! That changes everything! Well one thing is most definitely certain... it most certainly does **NOT.**

Heaven is the reward and God is the rewarder, now does that sound accurate? What type of Heaven or Lord do you envision that rewards the self inflicted? When is it ok to be convicted over and over by The Holy Spirit and instead of adhering to the promptings and signs he has given you, you resist him time and time again, until you don't hear him anymore. It's like the first time you smoke a cigarette or try marijuana and you feel bad inside, maybe a little worried, that is the spirit manifesting guilt to convict each naive soul of what is right from wrong. In other words the **LIGHT**. Or as Jesus would say in the book of *John 14:6 " I am the way, the truth, and the life."*

Trust me I know nobody is perfect, but I also know you don't have to be perfect to know right from wrong, or especially to hear the promptings of The **ALWAYS** faithful promptings of the always faithful Holy Spirit. I rest my case.

We can run but we can't hide, for God shines light in to even the darkest of places; our conscience. As hard as it is to believe, we do all have one of these, that way God can make certain we all are responsible for our free will, whether it seems like it or not. Trust me we are not duped, maybe stupid to believe we are, but in reality we are free and opened to choices with the ability to discern, so wise up! You can make all the excuses for the drunkard and drug addict, calling it love, (if that is you definition of love,) but that is not love, because love is a blessing.

Love is a battlefield not a prison. The best vision of love that I can give you is someone who was slain to set the captives free, and this is the thanks that He gets? Did anyone nurse His wounds or run to the battle zone in His defense? Absolutely **NOT**! So you tell me why should Christ run again to defeat this spirit of death we know to often as addiction? Is this not one of many principalities of darkness that Jesus already conquered, and of the reason he was slain? What more do you want from him? Wouldn't you be embarrassed if you lived your life perfectly for your children, were beaten and slain for them to conquer their death sentence of drugs, perversion, murder,etc, just to see your beloved children run right to it, and even be overtaken by this sin, even unto their own death? How would you feel knowing the same sin that killed your child, you had already defeated by your own life and death?

We all should be ashamed for being so unsightly! Instead of worrying when He will free you, did you ever think what bruising, beatings, lashings and whippings He sustained in being marked by your iniquity and shame? All for us to be able to live among the abominable, sorcerers, and God haters with assurity, the assurity that Christ gave, and the certainty that, **IT IS FINISHED!**

John 19:30

30 When Jesus therefore had received the vinegar, he said, It is finished: and he bowed his head, and gave up the ghost.

It is finished means just that. What has been said of Christ to that point was fulfilled. All is forgiven from the beginning, now to continue in this Justice and Assurity, we know Christ said "repent and be baptized for the remission of your sins."

Are you willing to be as the people who crucified Christ?

Hebrews 10:26-27

26 For if we sin willfully after that we have received the knowledge of the truth, there remaineth no more sacrifice for sins,

27 But a certain fearful looking for of judgment and fiery indignation, which shall devour the adversaries.

Choices, choices, choices, don't ever be the fool and let someone look you in the face and say they have run out of choices, (as many will try to do) and make way for them, because then their shame belongs to you. Don't think if you chase them away your giving way for them to use drugs or be ungodly. The destruction doesn't always come from the one chasing after them, but from the one they are running to, in some cases.

That final rebuke might just be the millstone they need to change as scripture says.

Luke 17:2-3

...2It would be better for him to have a millstone hung around his neck and to be thrown into the sea than to cause one of these little ones to stumble. 3Watch yourselves. If your brother sins, rebuke him; and if he repents, forgive him.

God is not a captive and the Holy Spirit is not for rent. God does not dwell among, or in sorcerers and definitely not among those who refuse to be set free, and choosing their self torture over surrender. For what more do they have to say to Christ when they choose the enemy over him? Where is the mercy you ask?

He might as well ask you the same question. And who considers the Lords feelings? Hasn't His body suffered enough?

Psalms 18:25-26

25 With the merciful thou wilt shew thyself merciful; with an upright man thou wilt shew thyself upright;

26 With the pure thou wilt shew thyself pure; and with the forward thou wilt shew thyself forward.

Revelations 22:11

11 He that is unjust, let him be unjust still: and he which is filthy, let him be filthy still: and he that is righteous, let him be righteous still: and he that is holy, let him be holy still.

Let me be clear that conflicted, afflicted, and self inflicted are three different substances. Now in saying that, you can be sure that one of the three afflictions, is a result of insubordination to the Courier of provisions, and self seeking in order to resolve His/her issues, resulting in even more serious issues including addiction, and even profound "self" existing, or desolation in laymen terms!

Who is God that he would fight against your free will? The Great Author of your free will, but not the authority of it, sorry He doesn't operate that way. Unless maybe you're a chosen host or spiritually among the Elected by the election of Christ or the God Head. Then refusal of improval, by submission to conviction, would make your life miserable, so greatly, that the only way one sees any hope or relief is submittal to **"repent or parish"** as a narrative, and not a lecture. Knowing nothing else will save you, and you're absolutely certain! That's the definition of a true captive on a slave ship, with no where to run, and ironically your own Savior is the one who owns the boat, is the captain of the boat, and is the master of the sea, by which the boat is steered and stays afloat! Now who runs things? Addicts now a days should be so lucky they still have a choice to change, because where I'm from, if you go astray seeking after your own provisions, your under the caption "sink or swim!" I hope that shows you a little insight to who I am, and who God says I am.

That's why I fight so hard, or maybe come off a little rough around the edges, and why shouldn't I be? If you know all the spiritual warfare I have been in, you could not, and would not, witness with a blind eye, nor your own understanding, because it doesn't exist, and I truly don't think it ever has, not even as "self existent", or "spiritually sleep" in other worlds. There's nothing wrong with being angry with the wicked, whether in this realm or the next, the Good Lord says he is angry with the wicked everyday! And the Lord is good and does no wrong!

Psalm 7:10-12

10 My defense is of God, which saveth the upright in heart.

11 God judgeth the righteous, and God is angry with the wicked every day.

12 If he turn not, he will whet his sword; he hath bent his bow, and made it ready.

Well my friend if your not angry with the soothsayers, the self righteous, self proclaimed and self ordained religious prodigals that preach indoctrinated man laws and not God's laws, if your not tired of the evil "me" generation that takes pride in the flesh and condones the ways of a very worldly world, and by the haters of God...if your not grieved at the fact that there is too much God to go around for these people not to have any of God in them, then I do believe you have your head screwed on backwards, because that's the only way that you can justify a backwards world!

How else are you going to justify the damnation of a God-fearing people who are true soldiers of God, acting as if we are the ones who should turn around. Well son we don't get our marching orders from you, or any other ungodly worldly creature! So who am I to be angry and what is my testimony? Sure I could tell you all about Katie McCreary, but I don't think that's what people are interested in as much as they are to learn what side of the dirt you come from and how many roots have grown that they can yank up, or dig up the bones the dog has buried in the process of "cleaning out the back yard" just to get one last chew at them, all while your tilling and turning over the soil to plant and sow a new seed. Trust me I've done my fair share of throwing dirt and hiding/exposing skeletons.

You see that's what's wrong with the world, everybody is so interested in one another, so focused on each other in the flesh, that they miss out on all of the spiritual focal points by the Great Creator, by not being focused on him. For me grace and mercy did **NOT** come cheap, and as others are using it for cheap measures and cheap gain, I will continue in professing His mercy through love, not only for each others love, (as most are only willing to produce love for,) but for sanctification and the renewing of the spirit through a sound mind and a heart that is more often forgotten in the ways of the world, and destitute when it comes to offering it up to God by unharmonious acts with the Spirit of God and illegitimate reform by the lack of knowledge. Knowledge is power! Without power the likely hood of you producing fruit is unmeasurable.

The Word of God came to me through hearing, by the spiritual milk and the solid food. Then God put a word in my mouth. Like I said I only take my marching orders from God, as no man in this world can testify with me as I stand in the presence of Holy God Almighty when I am absent from my body. So being that Jesus paid the price for my life, for this power that I may obtain, I don't have to sit on it as a crutch, I can use this same power that the Lord operates in, to operate under, and spend the rest of my God given life paying he that saves, back in fruit!

You create your own prison make no mistake about that. I'm here to witness to this. I told you I don't make the rules, I just make certain I follow them, that drugs nor addictions control me, and to know that I am not my own!

I said I would not make this about me, which would be easier to explain the hell I have been through and apart of, but that's another story. Which proves God does choose who he wants to, and that goes without saying. What backlash or ridicule would I conjure up if I didn't attest to that? Spare me would you? I'm not that easily offended. There's not an empty insult that I fear I couldn't forget or move forward from, so who's time are we wasting here? Where I go when I die, I have **ALL** day!

Moving along. God sends the Comforter to comfort. Why would God comfort the unruly in their sin? Does that sound like Him? God also sends the same Holy Spirit to offer inspiration, and guide you away from sin to repentance, isn't that the plan? Now listen, abominations are exceptionally different because they do not see any wrong in their relationships, (homosexuality) their professions (as in life styles) or careers, (FDA, CDC, ADA, and most importantly CIA. to name a few abominable professions) per status quo.

Let us talk about the practice and participation of the abominable for a brief moment. Right or wrong idol worship is a thing of ancient history, it's barbaric, and done and over with right? **Wrong - O!** Lets start by saying worship is the practice of participating in sacrificing one's own soul in religion or service to a higher power or religion God or Goddess. Idolatry is the object controlling the individual eminently, even to the degree of self sacrificing one's own soul to Satan subconsciously. Now where do you think anybody in their right mind would actually participate in idol worship? The answer is right in their own mind! Figuratively speaking. I guess it is true what they say, the mind is a terrible thing to waste, isn't it? Now you see idolatry doesn't always expose who their false God really is, even Christians low key worship Satan, and who would those perpetrators be? We all know the demigod of Christianity **"HO HO HO MERRY CHRISTMAS!"** or should I say Demi-anity? Holidays? What's **HO HO** Holy about them? Does the Easter bunny work for Yahweh or Yeshua? No way! Then why should our Savior who was brutally beaten and left crucified for humanity, nullify his **HOLY HOLY HOLY** days of sanctification and worship, that only He is worthy of, over determining who these people are truly worshipping? Are they that confused about who Satan is? He's the mastermind behind all masterminds and there's nowhere to run because he's everywhere.

Amos 5:21

21I hate, I despise your feast days, and I will not smell in your solemn assemblies.

These assemblies and feasts where all about money, and greed, and how much loyal change has the Lord witnessed in these prophesied evil generations? The results are staggering.

Proverbs 28:9

9 He that turneth away his ear from hearing the law, even his prayer shall be abomination.

I could see God and all His Heavenly Armies saying this verse in Isaiah to all the false gods/deities, to all the drug Lords, and those who practice this perverted sorcery and/or worship these images!

Isaiah 41:24

"Behold, you are of no account, And your work amounts to nothing; He who chooses you is an abomination."

Now many will come in with a back landish defense using the verse in Colossians.

Colossians 2:16

16 "Let no man therefore judge you in meat, or in drink, or in respect of an holyday, or of the new moon, or of the Sabbath days."

Let me first say these pagan holidays are **NOT** holy days on God's calendar, nor are they appointed by God. Most every American who knows the pagan holidays, could never observe any of God's appointed assemblies, because they are oblivious to all of them!

Second let me explain what this verse means as I had to study it and seek wisdom. The Holy Spirit revealed the translation of this paradigm as He stated to me in wisdom saying;

*"No human sacrifices are acceptable to the King and Lord our God, so he shames these things as municipal correlations between what sanctifies, heals, or saves. One reason is Judgement's Constable has all authority to judge intimately and not in regards to who participates and witnesses to what the Bible says is clean or unclean. He loathes **SELF** sacrifices and **SELF** righteousness.*

To this it rings true that iron sharpens iron, easily, but if you have the sharpest tool in the shed, then what are you witnessing for? Is it not like putting fire up to ice? Or does fire reduce fire?

An open mouth does get fed, but a closed mouth does not need feeding." Thus saith The Holy Confidant.

So in layman terms, those who know better do better, without boasting in their wisdom or works because neither one became of ones own self. This verse is sight to the unsightly, saying do not see a man as righteous for his works, or even something as preforming miracles, as this is self righteous peril. How can one man esteem another man by outward appearances of godliness? But in no way is this scripture giving way to the excuses a man may have.

Under the circumstances that the Lord himself delivers knowledge, wisdom, and understanding, standing in the gap for all lovers of knowledge, wisdom, and understanding, that they might nullify the law and entreat to each person of witness to the Lord's strong hand and solemn rebuke, to obtain knowledge accordingly for sanctifications, and enamored by the truth that saves us all.

2 Thessalonians 2:9-12

9 The coming of the lawless one is according to the working of Satan, with all power, signs, and lying wonders, 10 and with all unrighteous deception among those who perish, because they did not receive the love of the truth, that they might be saved. 11 And for this reason God will send them strong delusion, that they should believe the lie, 12 that they all may be condemned who did not believe the truth but had pleasure in unrighteousness.

John 9:41

"If you were blind," Jesus replied, "you would not be guilty of sin. But since you claim you can see, your guilt remains.

I understand we are not under the laws, but God is still the same, and if He hated it before; you can bet your bottom dollar that He hates it **STILL!** The Commandments will always remain.

Matthew 15:3 - But he answered and said unto them, Why do ye also transgress the commandment of God by your tradition?

Exodus 20

1 And God spoke all these words: 2 "I am the LORD your God, who brought you out of Egypt, out of the land of slavery. 3 "You shall have no other gods before me. 4 "You shall not make for yourself an image in the form of anything in heaven above or on the earth beneath or in the waters below. 5 You shall not bow down to them or worship them; for I, the LORD your God, am a jealous God

YOU SHALL NOT make for yourselves an image in the form of anything!

This includes Santa, drugs, sex, porn, money, etc. Do you want to know what all these have in common? They all reveal the lusts and desires of the heart. To tempt thine eye. Don't be so passive, the enemy has planned his agenda with mortual design, from the ancient day of the nomads, until time returns again to instinctively living as means of survival. Trust me this day will come...for **EVERYONE!**

What you will not tolerate, you will not provoke, but persistency is consistency! If your going to go toe to toe and head to head with the enemy, then you must know the achievements he has already progressed in innumerably, and his persistence of the intellectual decline of human intelligence spiritually, and physically, by the same power that's dragging us behind by the torches! I say torches because torches are sticks with combustible material at one end, which is ignited to burn as a light. The devil knows what he has is combustible, and with the same materials that he lights the way and leads people astray with, will inevitably lead us into darkness and burn us. (as drugs lead to sorcery and idolatry, and money leads to greed and envy, etc.)

Just as human sacrifices or services are offered up to a Holy God, as a human assembly or festival they call holidays, to be a holy day that is set apart. Acting like perfect families, perfect mothers, husbands, sons, and daughters, all for Christmas, when they should be behaving in such mannerisms always not putting on a act for each other. Then when they go back to their regular lives they love to use the defense that " nobody is perfect", because money and gifts truly do change people. Is God suppose to except that fakeness, that act as some sort of worship? If so then I guess God missed the memo! All God sees in so many people during Christmas is lovers of money, lovers of strong drink, gossip, gluttony, and spiritualism that God despises! With history that includes "Christ-mas" reindeer instead of The

Lamb and his sheep, and teachings of Santa instead of Satan. No rulers of darkness just "Christ-mas" elves, no crucifixion just a "Christ-mas" tree, and instead of a **HOLY-DAY** for atonement, these sacrilegious so called "God fearing" men and women want a **HOLIDAY** so they can be holly and jolly, with more Kris (Kringle) then Christ! I don't see Christ in any of this spoof! No one knows the exact day Christ was born or even exactly how old he was when he died, and not once in the Bible did Christ or any of even his closest followers, celebrate his "birthday" annually, nor did he instruct them to. So to help you see the enemies plan to suck you in to the worldly religions, and be conformed by the ways that provoke God to anger and jealousy, let me ask you; if you feel like setting time apart for the recognition of Christ, whether it be his birth, death, or both, then why would one share this beautiful time to honor God and his Son, with a make believe children's\ character? Do people worship their children so much that they put their fantasies and happiness before their own Savior? Second question, if you are adamant about having make believe in your children's life, then why of all days would you profess God on the same day as Santa or an Easter bunny or vice versa professing Santa or the Easter bunny on days you profess God? How is this ok with so called " God fearing" followers who claim to know God and love him, yet are breaking the commandments by this mockery, no matter how you look at it or what excuses you hold! It's derision and it's sacrilegious parody! Ironic isn't it, well I told you The enemy is the master of illusion.

Colossians 2:8 - Beware lest any man spoil you through philosophy and vain deceit, after the tradition of men, after the rudiments of the world, and not after Christ.

The enemy is in the drug dealing business you call pharmacy and pharmaceuticals you call medicine. But medicine is not what you think it is. Truth be told for every real religion there is a false religion, medicine is a false religion, not only a false religion, but also an occulted practice. So if you think you know what sorcery is think again! Pharmacy and pharmaceutical are derived from the Greek word pharmakeia (sorcery).

Do you have any idea why medicine is sorcery? Lets go back to Simon the sorcerer, he bribed the men with money in order to receive the power of the Holy Spirit.

Acts 8:18

18 When Simon saw that the Spirit was given at the laying on of the apostles' hands, he offered them money 19 and said, "Give me also this ability so that everyone on whom I lay my hands may receive the Holy Spirit."

20 Peter answered: "May your money perish with you, because you thought you could buy the gift of God with money! 21 You have no part or share in this ministry, because your heart is not right before God. 22 Repent of this wickedness and pray to the Lord in the hope that he may forgive you for having such a thought in your heart. 23 For I see that you are full of bitterness and captive to sin."

Now lets go back further to Adam and Eve. The Serpent persuaded Eve, that if she eats of the forbidden fruit and possessed what was of the fruit, she would then be like God having the power of the knowledge over good and evil. Yes that was the act of sorcery that took place in the garden of Eden! Instead of being obedient to God's command as his friends, they were rebellious, and God calls that witchcraft!

Adam and Eve became like Satan desiring to be like God, behind his back at that! They didn't seek His council or ask Him if they could share in what they were desiring from him, No! Instead they tried to posses His power through the aid of actions/gestures (in these cases fruit and money) in order to exercise or utilize supernatural powers, which is the exact definition of sorcery. The thing about sorcery is that it comes from the master of illusion himself the devil, and hardly ever does it look like sorcery! As you can see not many people will acknowledge that what took place in the Garden of Eden was sorcery, but that's also what the serpent didn't tell Eve, as he is the master of illusions! Sorcery is an abomination to God for these very reason, and all things that resembles sorcery. Modern day sorcery is called drugs whether you like it or not, **ALL** drugs! Many people will tell you that when they take certain drugs it makes them they feel closer to God, and they do things that they wouldn't normally do without the "high", If you worship God or go to church, and are kind to your friends and family only when you have your drugs, then you are practicing sorcery. This temporary energy, stamina, and love, God calls unnatural abhorring **"SIN-ERGY"** and is not of the Holy Spirit. It's hocus-pocus and must be repented of!

If you only knew how grotesque, abominable, and even perverted the demons of sorcery, witchcraft, murder, suicide, addiction, and blasphemy are, you would turn around with closed eyes and never look back! Believe me when I tell you one demon carries 7 more! God said repent of your sorceries. When you don't repent, you are rebelling, which God said is witch craft! So you are now practicing sorcery and witchcraft. Not only are drugs poison but they are spiritual and even physical suicide. So now you have the demon of sorcery, witchcraft, and suicide! The demon of suicide is also a demon of murder, not only of yourself but in your heart and towards others, especially Jesus Christ! I told you when you don't repent and obey Christ's Word, it is now you who crucifies Christ.

So many people have children living at home with them. Not only are they living with you at what is suppose to be their "home", they are now living with the demon of sorcery, witchcraft, suicide, and murder! Children and animals are very sensitive to the spiritual realm. I know from my own childhood, as well as the spiritual warfare I was under in my home, that my children and animals were greatly affected. Talk about a living nightmare and physical haunting! I lived with these same demons I mentioned for most of my life. How else do you think I know so much? I certainly cannot pull this reiteration out of my back side, as much as so many would hope. Afraid not. As with all drugs, there is an addiction demon that comes attached, working endlessly day and night seeking whom it may devour.

There are different forms of demons and different forms of serpents. Drugs come with demonic presences and rare forms of evil known as serpent-tilian in the demonic realm, they are a force like non other! Masquerading around in rare but oblique dimensions, (as a snake with abilities to coil around something) with peculiarity in ordinance by what rank they obtain, through the diminishing of one's own sight, in by which drugs happen to be where these demonic creatures are most notorious. It so happens that one cannot justify by reason, why a mark so peril in time would stand as an immediate referral to the under world, whence through time revealed the aspects from one's notion, can be greatly criticized by the moral standard of someone who holds all the knowledge of this particular subject, in which we are now regarding in particular as tyrannical drugs, under the power given to them through demonic manifestation of what people obviously consider "irrelevant" serpents, in which will soon be very relevant to man!

God showed me through photos that I had taken during my spiritual bind, capturing demonic entities by the grace and will of God, to show me the evil that comes with sin. Many times in these pictures there would be some grotesque looking object or creature coiling itself around one of us as a snake, I noticed the body of this serpent had the features of a crocodilian. I seen in another photo there was some sort of band over our eyes. In another photo my mom was smoking a cigarette, she said something was bothering her out on the porch. I took some pictures and there it was, a small frog like creature with a long tail that was wrapped around the arm of the hand she was smoking with!

I have received much knowledge and understanding for what I seen and experienced by the grace of God. God is the Truth and he will tell you the truth about your life!

Drugs carry heavy laden consequences you can be certain. Not only in the physical but also the spiritual, and not only in this life but the one to come. Serpents can manifest themselves through object, especially when it has been offered as a sacrifice or offering to a demon. Drug lords do this and they have a demonic ritual to lay the drugs they will be carrying in front of an idol and sacrifice it so the demon will "bless" it. Then either a demon or a serpent will manifest itself and enter the drugs. This keeps the drug lord and the drugs out of police hands, so to speak. In turn this evil spirit can now oppress and even posses a person who comes in contact with these drugs. Pretty scary stuff right? It's all very very **REAL**! Not all serpents have faces, but they still have poisonous venom, and if you consume them you will surly die imminently, it's inevitable!

I'm not here to condemn or tell anyone if you take medicine you will die or perish by the Lord. I was commanded by God to witness to the spiritual torment I endured, along with give a strong warning to those that have given their lives over to something other then God, because not only are they allowing something to control them, they are also making this idol "god" of their life. This does very much provoke Him to jealousy, which might proceed judgment or a terrifying rebuke!

The saying *" live by the sword, die by the sword,"* is a idiom and Jesus spoke about this in Matthew 26:52

52 Then said Jesus unto him, Put up again thy sword into his place: for all they that take the sword shall perish with the sword.

The truth is the truth and practicing medicine (drug use) is practicing a false religion, because what ever your illness or pain, God is still in the healing business and still very **ABLE**! People put their faith in medicine and hope in a miracle by a man made substance that comes with more warning labels and side effects then they know what to do with. When the most serious side effect being dealt, is the personal side effect being felt by God.

Why should The Greatest Healer and God who resurrects the dead, be pushed aside over sorcery, over man made medicine? Too many people are hoping and expecting from medicine, what they're suppose to be hoping and expecting from the Holy Spirit. The Helper is to help you, not to direct you to someone or something else for help. Very seldom does He direct any one, especially a true believer to seek medicinal resources for healing purposes, as He IS the great healer. Medical help is not medicinal, they are different, yet sorcery will pop up where ever it sees a opportunity. God is the Great Healer, yet drug/medicine causes dependency, addiction, unhealthy and even life threatening side effects! Does that sound like God, to induce and support torment? In no way is medicine a reflection of any of God's attributes in any form. God is the giver of life, while drugs take life and lives, that should tell you who or what these drugs operate under!

Peter said to Simon the sorcerer, " *may your money parish with you because you thought you could buy the gift of God with money.*" Many people are doing the same thing with medicine, trying to buy their healing or get God's supernatural gift of healing through substances. Sounds like cheating on God with the carnal mind (enmity against God) if you ask me.

Isaiah 59:1

1Behold, the LORD'S hand is not so short That it cannot save; Nor is His ear so dull That it cannot hear. 2But your iniquities have made a separation between you and your God, And your sins have hidden His face from you so that He does not hear.

Perhaps the reason for all these "side" effects come from the main source, and that's pushing God to the side. For every cause there is an effect. God cannot be mocked my friends.

Revelation 13:10

10 If anyone is destined for captivity, into captivity he will go; If anyone is to die by the sword, by the sword he must be killed. Here is a call for the perseverance and faith of the saints.

Galatians 5:19

19 Now the deeds of the flesh are evident, which are: immorality, impurity, sensuality, 20 idolatry, sorcery (pharmakeia), enmities, strife, jealousy, outbursts of anger, disputes, dissensions, factions, 21 envying, drunkenness, carousing, and things like these, of which I forewarn you, just as I have forewarned you, that those who practice such things will not inherit the kingdom of God.

Now tell me what benefits God to hope in the ungodly man or comfort the unsightly, illiterate, and abominable, who doesn't know right from wrong, or knows what's right and does not do?

Psalms 146:3 Put not your trust in princes, nor in the son of man, in whom there is no help.

Is God suppose to give them grace and give them over to riches and God's own heavenly treasures? Tell me one reason that God should allow someone who doesn't worship under His Heavenly abode, who doesn't recompense for all of Jehovah's Assembly, and most importantly doesn't listen to His Holy Helper, His Holy Spirit. Whether it's God the Father or God the Son or even if a someone thinks they are the same being, one thing you don't do is deny the Holy Spirit. This is a big **NO NO** that carries a heavy and ungodly consequence! Do you know what the consequence of this ungodly act is? Blasphemy to the Holy Spirit of The Loving God. Write that down I encourage you to as a friend! Many people think blasphemy to the Spirit of God is only speaking against him, but the truth is denying him in word or deed is under the same action and consequence. Yes blasphemy to the Spirit of God is holding on to any sin and resisting the convictions and promptings of the Holy Spirit. This blocks the working of God in our lives. Only God can judge the intentions of a man's heart, but the Bible does speak against this atrocity with a tumultuous rebuke!

2 Timothy 3:4-6

4 Traitors, heady, high-minded, lovers of pleasures more than lovers of God;

5 Having a form of godliness, but denying the power thereof: from such turn away.

6 For of this sort are they which creep into houses, and lead captive silly women laden with sins, led away with divers lusts,

Look around, the Only friend that is going to tell you the truth is someone who cares for you, knows you, fights for you, lived for you, died for you, and lives again forevermore, just for you. All so you can know Him, not the other way around! Where else can you find a friend that's half as patient, half as daring, and half of the man you never were (this is where wisdom would knock you back a bit if could understand this innuendo of half the man) Let me explain Him in size.

Father, Son, Holy Spirit. (just in case you lack in the wisdom category) Let me explain a little broader. The Father doesn't have to be half the man because the Father doesn't come down, The Holy Spirit doesn't come to be half the man you never were because that's non of his business where he's concerned. That leaves Yeshua, a friend, a helper, and a sacrifice for one man's sins that caused all men enmity and strife. Would you lay down your life for a fellow man just as Jesus? Just to be killed over and over and over by those who call you their friend and Savior? As you witness someone who calls for you day and night, who's very indebted to you, though you acknowledge that you have never known them, although they hope in you for some reason or the other. What the stigmata is, is this; a man can lean and cry upon your shoulder, but that doesn't make what he has done diminish or forgiven, when a man's open opportunity is to relinquish the cares of the world at the foot of the cross, and give He who saves the opportunity to do what He was born to do, save. You can't help someone who is inoperable. For the love of the flesh is destruction and enmity towards God. Is it better to love and lost then to never had the chance to experience love for the first time? Well confession, true love cannot be confounded. If true love is everything they say it is, then why is it so lost and never found? One of two reasons: it doesn't exist or it has never been found. In which we all would have a terminal sentencing if this were true! So in regards to Yeshua/Jesus being half the man you never were I ask you, if Jesus was made for you, why weren't you made for him?

1 Corinthians 6:13

Now the body is not for fornication, but for the Lord; and the Lord for the body.

1 Corinthians 6:19-20

19 Or do you not know that your body is the temple of the Holy Spirit who is in you, whom you have from God, and you are not your own? 20 For you were bought at a price; therefore glorify God in your body and in your spirit, which are God's.

"Because love isn't produced by the flesh, and we are the flesh" explains everybody. Oh really? Could have fooled me! Love became flesh, love died in the flesh, and love rose and resurrected in the flesh! As Jesus gave up the Ghost on the cross, and his body was also resurrected with him! So why doesn't love conquer? (I didn't say it wouldn't) But why doesn't it? Because man has to claim it! Doesn't that show you who love truly is? Love is who we honor. Not who we say we "honor". Woe unto these people!

Isaiah 29:12

12 Then the book will be given to the one who is illiterate, saying, "Please read this." And he will say, "I cannot read." 13 Then the Lord said, "Because this people draw near with their words And honor Me with their lip service, But they remove their hearts far from Me, And their reverence for Me consists of tradition learned by rote, 14 Therefore behold, I will once again deal marvelously with this people, wondrously marvelous; And the wisdom of their wise men will perish, And the discernment of their discerning men will be concealed.

As the question still inventively remains, what does the illiterate, unresponsive, abominable man produce that would benefit the godly? A stronghold? A reverence? Maybe a pictograph of the nations in all their turmoil, with having no regard to God or his disciples, while having loose barriers with their candidacy and paramount discrepancies in regarding the truth with inapplicable conduct, which is indulged in to serve and acquaint men together as bonafide subjects, where as to congregate with one another to serve in a self sinister battle of accomplishing power, by which holds no means of servitude to God as recognition for the adornment of this habeas nation and national scrutiny, and by no means do these "parliaments" care about the better well being of it's people! I tell you there is no hope for the abominable without repentance!

Isaiah 55:9

For as the heavens are higher than the earth, so are my ways higher than your ways, and my thoughts than your thoughts

The ways of the world are not the ways of God. What type of God would we be living for if they were? Scary thought! You may think America is a blessed nation by the hand of God, serving under his rule. That is a far cry from the harsh realities of the quivering truth. Maybe at one point in time this great nation was abroad, succulent in dispensaries that were catered to by the hand of the Great Elohim, but now a Just and Jealous God has turned back, covering his face from the sinful ways of this nation, that have reached up to him in his heavenly throne! What shame and despair we are facing when time reveals who has really been on our side! Im sorry but the proof is in the manuscript, and we as a nation have allowed America, who was a daughter to God and sister to Israel, to become a harlot, fornicating around on God, her first love. She has broken her seal by allowing foreign passengers to bombard her with expectations, ridicule, and a standard that allows them to play America for the fool. Do you think they are standing around singing kumbaya all day? **NO!** They're setting up mosques and grand juries, pushing Sharia Law to compromise the means of *"One Nation Under God"* and *"United We Stand, Divided We Fall"* Sound Historical? Well what doesn't is the ability to walk down the open road and be flagged down by a passer by who loathes your abilities and freedom, in which their "god" who they come to America to worship,(who they were more then free to worship in their own country) did not offer them the same respects of living and peace, because quite frankly their "god" doesn't exist. But they proceed to take your life claiming it is ungodly for Americans to live the way they do!

Can't argue with that aspect of their assumption, but no man should be allowed to take another man's life over religious differences!

The book of Daniel transcribes the exact fate of the harlot nations in all their ridicule and mockery of a Holy God, for it was Daniel who would bring forth judgments and prophesy in a king's dream.

Daniel 2:40-43

40And the fourth kingdom shall be strong as iron: forasmuch as iron breaketh in pieces and subdueth all things: and as iron that breaketh all these, shall it break in pieces and bruise.

41And whereas thou sawest the feet and toes, part of potters' clay, and part of iron, the kingdom shall be divided; but there shall be in it of the strength of the iron, forasmuch as thou sawest the iron mixed with miry clay.

42And as the toes of the feet were part of iron, and part of clay, so the kingdom shall be partly strong, and partly broken.

43And whereas thou sawest iron mixed with miry clay, they shall mingle themselves with the seed of men: but they shall not cleave one to another, even as iron is not mixed with clay

God has set Americans apart in many ways. Many people claim they don't know their calling by God, but when you were born in American you were born into your calling. Many have done nothing with their superior position in life! God bore America for freedom and for help, by the wealthy hand of God, but America refused the Great Giver, by choosing for herself a king that would love destruction, war, and fueling abominations! What tragedy to have no moral compass to live by, and going further and further away from the truth, from God. I am alarmed at the peasants and the beggars that surround the round tables of democracy, just trying to get what ever crumbs that may be handed over to them! And this is ok? Certainly this world is out of touch with their Master, and provisions are scarce. It's time to put the bottle down, open up the Book, and let's all get on the same page! This world is drunk with regrets, and staggering in abominations. This may be history, but this surely isn't **His**-tory! For **His** story redeems through forgiveness by sanctifying through repentance! That's why there is no hope for the abominable of this nation unless they repent!

(Notice I said this nation.) Judgement of this nation will be very personal, mark my words. For we have trespassed against God in a heinous most disrespectful way! To allow the worship of false gods cultivate our nation, and give us over to a non traditional society of immigrants that know no reason for the God we once loved and served. To pillage our people of the blessings we were set to receive in faithfulness, as hearty entreaties, gathering their rudiments as given to us by the founding fathers who were set in stone by their proverbial love for this nation!

The saying is true "time dwindles down to nothing" and the anarchy of one's soul is tumultuous in greed, but what their political solidarity is not saving up for, is room for grace!

Proverbs 13:24

Whoever spares the rod hates their children, but the one who loves their children is careful to discipline them.

Love isn't apart of who Christ is, love is Christ. In order to love Christ you have to love your brother with compassion, not with worldly passions like the homosexuals or the whoremongers who are also among the abominable. The only way your going to have salvation is to bind your life in Christ, because the Holy Spirit cannot explain to a foreigner the Kingdom's language, that would be like explaining childish things to a child of no words, and expecting good rapport. The scripture says in

1 Corinthians 2:13

…13And this is what we speak, not in words taught us by human wisdom, but in words taught by the Spirit, expressing spiritual truths in spiritual words. 14The natural man does not accept the things that come from the Spirit of God. For they are foolishness to him, and he cannot understand them, because they are spiritually discerned.

Romans 8:5-7

5 For they that are after the flesh do mind the things of the flesh; but they that are after the Spirit the things of the Spirit.

6 For to be carnally minded is death; but to be spiritually minded is life and peace.

7 Because the carnal mind is enmity against God: for it is not subject to the law of God, neither indeed can be.

Now I got to ask you, is Christ destined to sit on the Mercy Seat just to commiserate over and over for the foolish and ungrateful sinner? Tell me why then do they expect mercy and pardons as the foolish man does, instead of rewards and heavenly blessings? Nobody respects or honors Christ's sovereignty as King, instead they would rather compensate Christ for all his sufferings by telling everyone how gracious and merciful he is, instead of living according to the Word himself! What then does Christ have to offer the sinner who claims his righteousness by the works of his own faith, but pity?

Did it ever occur to you that these attributions are handed down as a gift to the one who knows him intimately, and not handed out as a system of who ever can get "close enough"? That's when people quit, when the feel like they're close enough on their terms, and the intimacy never forms. Did it ever occur to you that the decision of who deserves mercy by grace, isn't offered to a man by his works, but by he who gives mercy and is internally gracious? Hence my saying these attributions are handed down, as Christ's Father handed them down to Him on earth, He has them for eternity, as does every man who lives by these same gracious attributions.

Matthew 6:15 says, For if you forgive other people when they sin against you, your heavenly Father will also forgive you. But if you do not forgive others their sins, your Father will not forgive your sins. Jesus says we cannot receive what we are unwilling to give.

We **cannot** receive what we are not willing to give! Mercy is on a wide spectrum where I operate from, and mercy doesn't play the game of confidence in your own faith as salvation, as faith is a part God's grace and **NOT** thee grace that saves! It is through Christ by faith that saves, and it is why mercy is for "whom the bell tolls!"

"Any man's death diminishes me, because I am involved in mankind; and therefore never send to know for whom the bell tolls; it tolls for thee."- John Donne."

No man is an island unto himself. No one is self-sufficient; everyone relies on others. This saying comes from a sermon by John Donne

Did believers forget that Christ is our Lord, Savior, King, and also our brother?

He is just as much apart of the Body Of Christ as we are! Needless to say. So then isn't mercy also for Him, to Him, by Him? The scriptures teach us over and over as such; that when we are loving someone we are to love that person as our self (the body of Christ) and if we are scoffing or mocking someone, Jesus said we are not doing it to the person, but now to Jesus himself! Did Christ not command each believer to put on love or put on Christ every day so that we are now an extension of Him, and operating in the Body of Christ? Since Christ is our brother, our friend, our neighbor, and especially our **KING**, who walks among us, what has blinded our understanding and blocked the revelations of this wisdom? That we are to show Christ just as much mercy, love, compassion, and hospitality as did the men and women of the Bible! For Christ's sake people literally!

1 Peter 1:3

3 Blessed be the God and Father of our Lord Jesus Christ, which according to his abundant mercy hath begotten us again unto a lively hope by the resurrection of Jesus Christ from the dead.

We are to show God the same attributions He shows us! We are to bless him, honor him, give him praises, give him fellowship, love, compassion, time, kindness, friendship, a family, truth, light, recompense, hospitality, gifts, patients, prayer, (Jesus prays to the father for us, and the Holy spirit mediates and utters our groans to the Father!) perseverance, life, and Death! Now do you think He expects these thing from us, the true followers, but says " leave out mercy!"

Remember **EVERYTHING IS EVERYTHING**! What sets you apart from the rest? Do you want to be like all the rest? Because as far as I can see, this so called "new age faith," modern religion, once save always saved, sugar coating, ear tickling, ego grooming, prosperity seeking, false doctrine teaching, cherry picking, the Sabbath is Sunday having, boring no fire filled sermon preaching, backbiting, backslidden, heresy and gossip in the church, living under no discernment willing, worldly worship learning, secular music loving, untendered heart sounding, no ear hearing, no sight for the perishing, something called "love" bearing witness, is lonely and distraught, with no Savior as His own witness!

Now Maybe this song isn't about you, but if it is then you got some proving to do before His song **IS** about you! His Love song that is, everybody has a love song, are you going to let Christ write yours, or are you going to be crying in your beer, singing to the beat of your own drum?

Isaiah 56:10-12
His watchmen are blind,
They are all ignorant;
They are all dumb dogs,
They cannot bark;
Sleeping, lying down, loving to slumber.
11 Yes, they are greedy dogs
Which never have enough.
And they are shepherds
Who cannot understand;
They all look to their own way,
Every one for his own gain,
From his own territory.
12 "Come," one says, "I will bring wine,
And we will fill ourselves with intoxicating drink;
Tomorrow will be as today.

The Lord gave me a very personal message about this mercy that he is worthy of and I ask at this time that you ask God to open and prepare your heart to receive these words that the Lord spoke to me saying;

*"I have delivered you out of the snares because you are worth it to Me. I have given you all of Me, but you turned your backs. **YOU MUST REPENT**! I have given you multitudes the chances to know me, but still no truth remains apart*

*from the foregoing's of the elected faithful servant. **I AM** under precise scrutiny by whom **I AM** loved, to bear witness for the lame, the ones bruised by iniquity, to relinquish My love for those starving for knowledge of the truth. I serve as a witness, as a grand juror to recompense and compensate for the just man I became apart of and not apart from. **I AM** the leader who knows no boundaries, and **I AM** set in My ways. I give notion to the ocean, and sight across the sea. **I AM** wonderfully made amongst My people. Now serve Me with recompense My restitution! **I AM** not given a reward on behalf of your explanations, I need truth! I desire truth! Now fuel Me for your husbands and children, for your wives and singled out cousins, who are in deep despair, over relinquishing your love on material monopolies, and desire for one's own soul necessities! I hold all the power to disguise your fate behind one another, and an empty curtain call is all I get in regards to fashion? What a clean slate. So clean I can only see My self in it. Is fate, that I must walk alone? Through all your derision, as fortitude? Am I mistaken like that? Am I mistaken as so? **I AM** not your worth **I AM** your mirth? Disguised to entertain? Well no more will I be the brunt of your joke. You have laughed and been merry for far to long. Now you must tender your hearts to endure the pain for the blood shed in many nations. I must teach you not to hold back in suffering, not to diminish amongst the strongholds and derision, and not to tarry in peacemaking with your brother and your neighbor. **I AM THE LORD!** Your hearts may be broken, but they were not made to shoot the fiery darts of man kind unto surrender. **I AM THE KING!** I will take no slackers, I will hold back My bow and My spear any longer. I will shake the mountains and the* *foundation for where they undermine me! I will take hold the pillow and the throw for the ones who want to sleep on My recompense! I will not rest."*

Thus says the Lord thy God.

SECTION NINETEEN

Mercy, Mercy, Mercy

Hasn't Christ suffered more then enough? Not only in His flesh, but now in the body of Christ, the church as some say. We all know His church is suffering to this great apostasy. Yet God is eternally merciful, and perfect mercy is completely rhetorical. Mercy is suppose to come back to God in the form of faith, trust, surrender, repentance, solitude, gratitude, thanksgiving, and good fruit. When we know Him we are suppose to pay Him back in fruit. That surly isn't much to ask of anyone who claims to love Him.

Think about grapefruit, it looks pretty appealing, but in order to reap any of the benefits it involves a little more then just what the eye can see. It involves taking a bite. To some people grapefruit has a bad taste, so even if they're sick they would rather purge on other fruits, then this one powerful super fruit for all their sickness.

The enemy whispers lies to convince you that you have so many challenges like depression, and anxiety, and a long list of sultry objects in your way to hinder or impede on your grace. The enemy doesn't want us to stand on God's grace or to be still and know that he is God. God wrote the book on His mercy and grace, so you would know your place. Even if the ground shook beneath you; you would not. The enemy wants you to believe mercy and grace comes at the end, but actually it's just the beginning. Seeing isn't always the angle of perceiving truth and reality. Hope serves as a better lens then the actual "eye of the beholder."

And as the idiom goes "make the money don't let the money make you."

We can always switch it around from ill reform to rich reform. Instead of money, milk and honey. With God's grace and mercy we can always see the glass as half full instead of half empty, or to some they are drinking from their saucers because their cups truly are overflowing! God truly is faithful to the faithful. Faithful isn't just a award it's who we belong to.

His mercy is power to worship.
His mercy is sanctification to praise Him.
His mercy is strength to come as you are.
His mercy is courage to surrender.
His mercy is peace from among the dead.

Now you tell me that a power like that doesn't deserve to be returned!

Mercy isn't the power to trust Him for the forgiveness of your sins, that's faith.

Mercy is the power to conquer sins and confess Him in the process! Now that's perfect mercy, right where it began! What a friend we have in Christ, a witness to no witnesses' end. Now that's Mercy!

SECTION TWENTY

SEEK

Matthew 6:33 " But seek ye first the kingdom of God, and his righteousness, and all these things shall be added unto you."

Hebrews 11:6 "And without faith it is impossible to please him: for he that cometh to God must believe that he is, and that he is a rewarder or them that diligently seek him."

James 4:8 " draw near to God, and He will draw near to you."

If you only seek the knowledge of God from the scriptures you might miss him in your life. God lives on the insole of your righteous man. The only time He is going to come though evidently, is if you take your time to search for Him.

God is a correlating spirit at work in our hearts. Did you know that the heart is the second arm to reach Him? The heart is the soul that masquerades within you pretending that it wants what it wants, like separating people by skin color or people from Christ. Yet the heart can be stolen. It's called a spiritual rapture, and it's the spiritual indwelling.

With wings like eagles, thy heart belongs to God.

Isaiah 40:30-31

…30Though youths grow weary and tired, And vigorous young men stumble badly, 31Yet those who wait for the LORD will gain new strength; They will mount up with wings like eagles, They will run and not get tired, They will walk and not become weary.

Whether we see his face or not, when we seek him, the turn around is always wonderful because someone is always watching!

Epilogue

Jeremiah 29:13 " And ye shall seek me, and find me, when ye shall search for me with all your heart."

Being scriptural and being spiritual are to different elements, just as seeking God and actually finding God are not one in the same; as they should be.

Everything is everything, so God is the living scriptures, yet it is not the text or literature alone that saves us personally. As in a food chain, God feeds whoever is close enough to him. You can't get fat if you merely just read scripture, you might even loose weight! For who are those who have fallen by the wayside? The scriptures combined with His voice allows us to go to perfection and not perdition, now that's satisfying!

Hebrews 6:12 " We do not want you to become lazy, but to imitate those who through faith and patients inherit what has been promised."

In fact *Hebrews 5:12* says *some of you have been believers so long now that you ought to be teaching others*! Instead you need someone teaching you again the basic things about God's word, and you are like babies(slothful, and lazy) who need milk and can not eat the solid food(voice of the Holy Spirit) of God.

We will always need the Word, but God's purpose of making the Word alive to us by the power and voice of the Holy spirit, is for us to obtain, not only the thirst (for milk) but the hunger (solid food) of maturing men and not as babies!

We are to taste His word's like meat and know they are good! This is what it means to truly seek Him diligently in faith, honor Him in his wisdom, and worship Him in spirit and in truth.

There is more then controlled religions want you to know, and it's that GOD IS!

Hebrews 11:6 "But without faith it is impossible to please him: for he that cometh to God must believe that he is, and that he is a rewarder of them that diligently seek him."

SECTION TWENTY TWO

Personal Messages From God.

So many people are afraid to seek out a personal God, because of religions, spirituality, and misconstrued beliefs. This exhausts people, and they give up before they start. I believe with all my being that God is a God who speaks to our own hearts for our personal growth, and not just for us to keep the gift of wisdom and knowledge to ourselves, but to minister to as many people as we can reach through another gift which is extraordinary faith. The word says in Isaiah God's word will not return to him void.

Isaiah 55:11

So shall my word be that goeth forth out of my mouth: it shall not return unto me void, but it shall accomplish that which I please, and it shall prosper in the thing whereto I sent it.

When we are taught by the grace of God, a unrelenting responsibility comes with it. Many who have received the knowledge of the truth by hearing God's voice know how compelled they are by the Holy Spirit's nudges and impression on our hearts to share with anyone who will listen. I use to think I had to convince people to believe in God or that he speaks first before they would ever believe that the words I was claiming he spoke were just as true. Thank God that once we truly know the truth that *his yolk is easy and his burden is light, (Matthew 11:30)* we can count on God to give the increase, and knowing all we are responsible for is planting the seed.

1 Corinthians 3:6-8

6 I planted the seed and Apollos watered it, but God made it grow. 7 So neither he who plants nor he who waters is anything, but only God, who makes things grow. 8 He who plants and he who waters are one in purpose, and each will be rewarded according to his own labor.

As I was in fellowship with God He spoke saying:

"**I AM** *who I say I AM*

I AM *not rude or angry*

I AM *a real gentleman*

I AM *your helper*

I AM *not helpless*

I AM God whether I sit or stand

test Me, search Me, try Me.

I AM worth it.

I AM more then ceremonial churches and heresy.

If you show up, I will show up, I will show you what I bring to the table.

I AM musically inclined, I do not always seem so scriptural.

Is it really about where I come from that keeps you alive to me?

I go where I go, I come from where I come. What is wrong with that?

Does My right hand not extend the way yours does, signaling loves first step?

If you find Me, I have no problem telling you everything.

Your greatest heart's harkening will never go ignored.

This is My promise to fulfil your mind, body, and soul, with total recompense.

I promise it is not as hard as it looks to find a friendship right here.

It could not be wrong when it is over and done. (when your life is over on earth)

As sure as you take your last deep breath, I will be right inside of you.

I know where I come from, and I know where humans come from.

If humans are created of the dirt, then is there anything in which I can not heal them from? Then can I not know My own children like a Father should? Can I not have a fair trial without getting stoned?

All I want is a fair chance to prove every miracle to you myself, that otherwise you could only witness to by scriptures. My beloved. I love My honor (My Word)

but it will only do for you what you let it. You can paraphrase, but you will not enhance the word unless the scriptures rub you the right way, and rings true for more then just a story in ancient time. Otherwise your dreams of gaining knowledge on a spiritual level will not happen. If you only look for Me in scripture, you are cheating yourself a whole relationship and revelations that enhance scriptures.

Search Me in your darkest hours. Search Me in the bottom of your doubts.

I will come! Trust in Me I will come gallantly!

__I AM__ exceptional

__I AM__ very personal

I AM proud like a proud Father at the smallest steps and first steps, or your first time calling My name, no matter what kind of situation we may be in.

I gave you all My personal introductions from the day I said "Let there be light!"

When you see all I have done in creation, does that not say "hello?"

Does it not witness to who I AM?

You do not have to rival with the sea, who knows and obeys Me, for My attention.

I AM right where I AM.

I promise it is not as hard as it looks to find a friendship right here.

Wherever you are in your life, that is where I will be, it is where I have always been, bit by bit, minute by minute."

said the Lord.

A message from the Lord on lukewarm believers, when I was also lukewarm He spoke with me saying:

"Katie, people are transforming genders like you wouldn't believe and truly believing that is who they are! But you lukewarm Christians will not give your life to Me and be

made a new creation because you do not believe. If you think it is easier to be a transgender then a new creation, you must be sleepy! Where is the confidence that He raises the dead, mentally and physically? A true repented sinner is not blind to the blasphemy, even among our own brothers and sisters in Christ. A true repented sinner does not need bribery to believe in God's unchangeable Spirit. He is not for rent! If Proverbs and Psalms are not encouraging enough, then you do not believe in diddly but smoke and mirrors.

Get thee away from me child of Satan, you are only a blessing for the dead." said the Lord.

God gave me the understanding.

He is saying the lukewarm Church is to often having a form of godliness but denying the power within. If we are not operating in the power of the spirit then we are only allowing the dead to do what they want walking in their own will, instead of being witnesses of the power and transformation by His Holy Spirit. Hardly will the lukewarm minister to the dead, let alone minister by the power of the Spirit who convicts. If we continue being lukewarm the Lord says He will spit us out of His mouth!

Revelations 3:16

So then because thou art lukewarm, and neither cold nor hot, I will spew thee out of my mouth.

Hence the statement He made *"get thee away from me child of Satan!"* If we stand around calling ourselves saved by our own self righteousness then we are allowing the dead to bury their dead.

Will their blood be on your hands?

Ezekiel 3:18

When I say unto the wicked, Thou shalt surely die; and thou givest him not warning, nor speakest to warn the wicked from his wicked way, to save his life; the same wicked man shall die in his iniquity; but his blood will I require at thine hand.

I didn't write this book over night, actually this book is made up of my personal solitude and fellowship with God and his Holy Spirit over the last six years starting in October 2011. I understand not everyone is where I am on their own personal journey with God, but encourage everyone to keep an open mind and take everything with a grain of salt because God is a God of many, and no one relationship with him is the same. When God spoke to me about writing he told me to share his heart and story with people, as God poured his own heart into mine. I understand this was a personal experience with my Father, but not to be kept hidden away in my heart, as His heart is now mine and He is a generous giver to those who ***seek*** Him.